Stethoscopes and Sacrifices

The Economic Front of Nigerian Medicine

by
Jwanna Savoie Powell, MT AAB, EOLD and Kingsley I. Anierobi, MD

Table of Contents

Introduction

Welcome to a pivotal exploration into a subject that touches the core of human dignity and progress—the healthcare system in Nigeria and the salaries of the doctors working tirelessly within this system. This exposé aims to shed light on a topic that is both urgent and deeply complex. It's a narrative that interweaves the lives of healthcare professionals with the very fabric of a society's well-being. Stripped of adequate resources, Nigerian healthcare stands at a crossroads, seeking paths of resilience and reform.

The health of a nation's citizens can be considered a lens through which to view its strength and stability. Unfortunately, for many in Nigeria, this lens reveals a fragmented system fraught with inadequacies. It is a topic that doesn't merely warrant a second glance; it demands a deep dive into the root causes, current challenges, and hopeful possibilities for the future.

Through this book, we endeavor to take you through the realities of the Nigerian healthcare landscape. Our focus is twofold: firstly, to inform on the deplorable state of healthcare in the country, and secondly, to bring to the forefront the circumstances surrounding the remuneration of its doctors—a critical element in any healthcare system's functionality.

The narrative of Nigerian healthcare is not just about statistics and policies; it's also about people. The doctors who navigate these turbulent waters are the protagonists in our story. Their resilience despite abysmal salaries speaks of a dedication that transcends financial rewards. However, the personal cost of such commitment remains high, leading many to seek greener pastures abroad.

As we move through these chapters, we will not simply recount facts. We aim to breathe life into the numbers and to craft a tapestry that reflects the lived experiences of those within the Nigerian healthcare sector. The tales are sometimes heartbreaking, often inspiring, but always speaking to the critical need for change.

Nigerian doctors face a Sisyphean task. Each day is a testament to their unwavering commitment, as they confront a litany of obstacles, including equipment shortages, infrastructural degradation, and an overwhelming patient load. Their salaries, neither commensurate with their skill nor their sacrifice, raise profound questions about the valuation of healthcare work in the nation.

This is not solely an academic discussion; the stakes are painfully real. The departure of medical talent from Nigeria creates a vacuum that further weakens an already struggling system. It's a story of loss and the ripple effects of brain drain, which poses severe consequences not just for the health of individuals but for the entire country's future.

We will explore the stark contrasts between urban centers and remote rural areas where healthcare can seem like a distant mirage. The disparity speaks to a broader narrative of inequality, where location predicts the likelihood of survival. It's a disparity that is unsustainable in the long run and bespeaks the silent emergencies happening away from the limelight.

As we dissect the patient-to-doctor ratio in Nigeria, the strain on the system becomes palpably clear. An overburdened workforce translates to compromised patient care—a domino effect that no society can afford. The repercussions of this strain are felt in every corner of the healthcare system, from policy-making to bedside manners.

The question of how to rejuvenate a failing system looms large. Government and bureaucratic challenges weave through the narrative, presenting a complex puzzle of mismanagement and missed opportunities. Corruption tarnishes aspirations for better healthcare, and we will delve into how this troubling factor thwarts progress.

Amidst these trials, technology offers a beacon of hope, a bridge towards innovation that could leapfrog the existing gaps in diagnosis and treatment. Still, the potential of these technological advances remains, for many, just out of reach. Identifying these limitations is one thing, but striving for tangible benefits is quite another.

Nigerian doctors' personal stories reveal a daily reality of making do with less, of sacrifice on an almost unimaginable scale. It's in these narratives that the truest forms of heroism are found—not in dramatic gestures, but in the quiet perseverance in the face of adversity.

Medical misdiagnosis is another layer of complexity that undermines healthcare efficacy. Our journey will unveil the causes of these misdiagnoses and seek strategies to mitigate them. Comprehending this issue is critical because every misdiagnosis weaves a thread of distrust in the healthcare tapestry.

The pharmaceutical sector in Nigeria suffers from its own ailment—access and affordability issues compounded by the peril of counterfeit medications. Our exploration into the import dependence and local production challenges will highlight how medication has become a double-edged sword that cuts deep into the fabric of societal health.

We will also consider the role of partnerships and international aid, scrutinizing their effectiveness in patching the holes within the healthcare system. While foreign assistance and NGOs play significant parts, determining their long-term impact is essential in moving towards sustainable health models for Nigeria.

This book sets out not just to inform, but to ignite discourse and ultimately, to inspire a movement towards actionable change. The fabric of Nigerian healthcare may be frayed, but it is within our power to mend it. By understanding the complex interplay between doctor salaries and the broader healthcare context, we can begin to envision a future of well-being and dignity for all Nigerians.

Chapter 1:
A Diagnosis of Nigerian Healthcare

In the shadow of Nigeria's bustling cities and under the canopy of its rural landscapes lies a healthcare system that's silently imploding. It's a narrative too common, yet profound in its implications. Throughout the country, the state of hospitals and clinics tells a story of decline: creaky beds in overcrowded wards, lifesaving equipment that remains perpetually out of reach, and dilapidated structures that hardly inspire confidence in the sick seeking solace within their walls. Overwhelmed physicians navigate these challenges daily, their stethoscopes and skills standing defiant against a tide of systemic neglect. The very fabric of the nation's healthcare is frayed, torn in spots where the threads of support and sustenance are thinnest. This chapter seeks to unravel the plight, examining not just the veneer of functionality but peering deeply into the core where the heart of Nigerian healthcare beats irregular and faltering, setting the stage for a profound understanding of just how critical the condition is.

The State of Hospitals and Clinics

As we zoom in on the current state of hospitals and clinics in Nigeria, a troubling picture comes into focus. These establishments, meant to serve as sanctuaries of healing, stand as stark symbols of a healthcare system in dire straits. The halls of many health institutions echo with the scarcity of vital medical supplies; often, the very lifeblood of effective healthcare delivery isn't there when it's needed most.

Ventilators, incubators, and even the most basic diagnostic tools are spread thinly across the country, sometimes non-existent in rural clinics where they're needed desperately. It's a rare but telling sight to see a fully equipped emergency room in public hospitals; more often than not, patients are turned away or face long waits, risking their lives as the hands on the clock ignore their pleas for help. These dire conditions paint a grim backdrop against which Nigerian doctors must somehow toil not just to practice medicine, but to perform what often seem like daily miracles. The wages they earn for their Herculean efforts, however, are grossly inadequate, compounding the challenges and feeding into a vicious cycle of brain drain and demoralized workforces that further hollows out the quality of care patients receive.

Resources and Equipment Shortages

The narrative of healthcare in Nigeria is frequently one of paradoxes: boundless potential met with stifling challenges, and none more significant than that of resources and equipment shortages. Nigerian hospitals and clinics are often caught in a quagmire of insufficient supplies, which has a cascading effect on the quality and availability of care provided.

Delving into the state of healthcare resources across Nigeria reveals a fractured landscape. While some urban centers may boast relatively modern facilities, many hospitals, particularly in rural areas, grapple with the lack of basic medical devices—from stethoscopes to blood pressure monitors. These deficiencies aren't just inconvenient; they potentially cost lives.

In the corridors of even the best-funded Nigerian clinics, one might encounter the stark reality of equipment rationing. With only a limited number of operational machines, such as X-ray or ultrasound machines, healthcare providers must make difficult choices about which patients receive diagnostic testing and when. This can lead to delayed diagnoses and treatments, ultimately harming patient outcomes.

Consider the plight of a small-town clinic, constrained by economic limitations and remote location, where a solitary, overworked centrifuge serves a population in the thousands. An unassuming piece of machinery, yet vital, becomes emblematically reflective of the healthcare system's broader predicament. When it fails, access to basic laboratory testing—an essential diagnostic tool—collapses.

Shortages extend to the very fabric of hospital operations. Personal protective equipment (PPE), crucial for maintaining sanitary conditions and preventing the spread of infections, often runs perilously low. The pandemic has harshly underscored this fragility, with countless healthcare workers facing increased risk of exposure due to inadequate protective gear.

Surgical capacity is hamstrung by the scarcity of anesthetics, sterile instruments, and even reliable electricity to power operating theaters. These harsh realities are compounded by the need to make do with aging or even faulty equipment; the integrity of the entire surgical process is thus compromised, resulting in postponed surgeries and heightened infection risks.

Pharmaceutical shortages add another layer of complexity to patient care. Vital medications, such as antibiotics and anti-malarials, are often in short supply, pushing patients to seek remedies in the unregulated, and frequently unsafe, informal market. The impact on public health is twofold: a rise in drug-resistant infections and a detrimental reliance on counterfeit or substandard medicines.

Moreover, the equipment that is available is often outdated, and the training to use contemporary technologies is sparse. Medical professionals are thus frequently unprepared to leverage the full range of capabilities that newer, more advanced equipment can offer, assuming such tools are even accessible.

Even the all-important ambulance services are plagued by resource shortages. The scarcity of well-equipped ambulances, coupled with poor road conditions, yields a precarious system incapable of reliably responding to emergencies. The golden hour—the critical period following traumatic injury or the onset of acute illness—often goes unmet, with fatal consequences.

Vaccine storage illustrates another instance of how equipment inadequacies directly influence public health. Without reliable refrigeration, the cold chain is disrupted, leading to vaccine spoilage and the consequent vulnerability of populations to preventable diseases. Immunization campaigns suffer, undermining global efforts to control and eliminate infectious diseases.

Investments in healthcare infrastructure might be perceived as a remedy, but without addressing the issues of maintenance and sustainability, even new equipment becomes quickly dated and joins the ranks of its unusable predecessors. The challenge, thus, extends beyond procurement; it's a complex dance of logistics, training, and upkeep.

Maintenance of medical equipment is another overlooked travesty. The broken, often non-existent, systems for repair and upkeep render even the most advanced technology ineffectual. A life-saving dialysis machine, immured in disrepair due to a lack of technical know-how or spare parts, epitomizes this sorry state of affairs.

Amid these shortages, the ingenuity and resilience of Nigerian healthcare workers shine through. Juggling multiple roles, they innovate makeshift solutions to sustain patient care. Yet, such resourcefulness, while admirable, is a clear signpost of systemic failure that should never be normalized or accepted as the status quo.

The implications of these shortages for doctors are profound. Physicians often find themselves unable to practice to the standards they were trained for, leading to frustration and, for some, the decision to practice elsewhere. This brain drain further depletes the healthcare system of skilled professionals, escalating the crisis.

Resources and equipment shortages in Nigerian healthcare are matters that can no longer afford to be relegated to the peripheries of policy discussion. They demand center stage, immediate attention, and decisive action. Without this, the hopes of a robust Nigerian healthcare system capable of adequately serving its citizenry remain a distant dream.

Infrastructure Challenges

While the previous section delved into the critical shortages of resources and equipment, we now turn our attention to the crumbling infrastructure within Nigerian hospitals and clinics, symbolizing deeper systemic malaise. It's no secret to those traversing the healthcare landscape in Nigeria that the condition of numerous healthcare facilities is not what it should be. The structures that house hope and healing are themselves in need of urgent care.

Step into any number of these facilities, and you're likely to encounter buildings deteriorating from neglect and an environment ill-suited for modern medical practices. It's not just about aesthetics; the physical state of these buildings poses significant risks to health and safety. Leaking roofs, cracked walls, and even instances of electrical failures create a setting that is far from the sterile enclave patients expect and, indeed, deserve.

This waning infrastructure is not a surface-level issue but is symptomatic of underlying corrosion within the nation's healthcare system. Many hospitals are overcrowded, with patients often spilling into hallways and even making shift outdoors. This not only compromises patient privacy and dignity but also disrupts efficient workflow for healthcare providers, exacerbating the already strenuous conditions under which doctors operate.

Accessibility is another critical component of infrastructure that remains woefully inadequate. Those with disabilities often find it near impossible to navigate the architectural constraints of medical facilities. In an era where inclusivity should be top of mind, this oversight further entrenches disparity in healthcare delivery.

Transportation, the backbone of any functioning system, is another area rife with challenges. Ambulances and other emergency vehicles are scarce, and those that exist are often in poor condition, making the timely transport of patients a Herculean task. When minutes can mean the difference between life and death, this is a gap that can't be ignored. Imagine the distress of those who must tackle this logistical nightmare in moments of absolute vulnerability.

The lack of consistent electricity and water supply is a significant barrier to operations in hospitals. Rather than a steadfast reliance on public utilities, many healthcare facilities are forced to resort to generators and water tanks as backups, which come with their own set of reliability and financial burdens. In an environment where sterilization and the preservation of life-saving medicines at controlled temperatures are crucial, these challenges become not merely inconvenient but potentially life-threatening.

In regions where healthcare facilities do manage to have sophisticated medical equipment, the lack of regular maintenance and technical expertise represents yet another hurdle. Equipment lies idle, gathering dust as the wait for repairs stretches from days into months. This is not only a loss of investment but also a denial of essential services that could save lives.

Data management systems—critical for effective patient care and administrative efficiency—are largely non-existent or archaic in many Nigerian healthcare institutions. Inefficient record-keeping has ramifications extending from patient care continuity to the ability to formulate effective public health strategies. Paper-based systems still dominate, fraught with issues of storage, security, and accessibility.

The shortage of sufficient and secure drug storage facilities leads to stockouts and compromises the quality of medicines. Without proper storage conditions, drugs can deteriorate or lose potency, undermining the very treatments that patients desperately need.

Waste disposal is yet another concern, with many healthcare facilities lacking adequate systems to safely dispose of medical waste. This not only endangers the environment but poses significant health risks to patients, staff, and the broader community through potential exposure to infectious and hazardous materials.

Moreover, many Nigerian hospitals lack adequate isolation rooms, which became glaringly evident during disease outbreaks such as Ebola and the ongoing COVID-19 pandemic. Infection control in general is a critical problem aggravated by insufficient infrastructure. This lack of isolation capacity can lead to the cross-contamination of patients, further straining an overburdened healthcare ecosystem.

The issue of security cannot be overstated. Hospitals need to be sanctuaries of safety, yet stories abound of facilities where patients and staff are at risk of theft or even violence. The lack of security measures contributes to the anxiety of healthcare workers and deters patients who might otherwise seek treatment.

In the midst of these challenges, Nigerian doctors remain undeterred, often working miracles in the least conducive of settings. These healthcare heroes operate with a resolve that is as admirable as it is heart-wrenching. Yet, the critical question remains: how long can these professionals be expected to compensate for the failings of infrastructure before they too are swallowed by the spreading cracks?

To drive improvements, there is a need for immediate and sustained investment in infrastructure, paired with a focus on regular upkeep and refurbishment. It's integral that this encompasses not just the physical buildings but the underlying support systems—electricity, water, transportation, data management, and security—that enable facilities to function optimally.

Addressing these infrastructure challenges is, without a doubt, a complex endeavor. It requires concerted effort from government, the private sector, and international partners. Investment in healthcare infrastructure is investment in the nation's future, as a robust health system will enable Nigeria to harness the full potential of its citizens and pave the way for a healthier, more resilient society.

Chapter 2:
The Lives and Livelihoods of Nigerian Doctors

Having peeled back the layers to reveal the state of healthcare facilities in Nigeria, our attention now pivots to those at the heart of the system—the doctors. Laboring under the weight of inadequate support and dwindling resources, Nigerian doctors navigate a precarious landscape. Their training, intense and thorough, belies the systemic frailties that leave them underequipped and frequently underappreciated. The financial compensation they receive, hardly a reflection of their crucial role, falls dismally short of global benchmarks. With salaries often delayed or inadequate, it's a testament to their dedication that hospital wards haven't fallen silent altogether. Yet, this chapter isn't simply about decrying their plight—it's a signal of untold resilience amid the tempest, a testament to their commitment to delivering care in spite of a cascade of disincentives. The livelihoods of these professionals, bound tightly to the health of a nation, are stories of unspoken struggles and unwavering hope, navigating a path few would choose, yet one they tread daily for the betterment of their countrymen.

Training and Faltering Support Systems

In the landscape of Nigerian healthcare, the journey of a doctor is fraught with a series of systemic hurdles, beginning with the foundational aspect of their career: their training. Medical education in Nigeria, a country with over 200 million individuals, is both a privilege and a formidable challenge. The underpinning support systems meant to shore up the learning process of these fledgling medical professionals are in a precarious state, often teetering on the brink of functionality.

Prospective doctors delve into an educational odyssey that's supposed to prepare them for the multifaceted challenges of healthcare delivery. They enter medical schools that are grappling with overcrowding, a consequence of the nation's burgeoning population that far outpaces the available institutional space. While the grit and determination of these students are commendable, one can't ignore the strains they face in under-resourced and often understaffed academic environments.

Moreover, the quality of training and clinical exposure that a medical student receives in Nigeria varies widely. Some institutions boast more sustainable facilities, but many others face scarcity that directly impairs the educational standards. The scarcity isn't merely of physical resources but extends to the availability of knowledgeable faculty to guide and mentor the next generation of doctors. This disparity in training quality creates a chasm between the theoretically sound and the practically astute.

There's also the weight of financial pressures. The costs associated with medical training are not insignificant, and with the Nigerian economy's fluctuations, families and sponsors of medical students can find the financial burden hard to bear. Despite their pivotal role, government scholarships and financial aid for medical students are sporadic at best, leaving many to rely on loans or family support that is not always guaranteed.

Clinical rotations, which should be a cornerstone of medical training, bringing theory to life, stand compromised. Medical students frequently report a lack of standardized protocols and seldom receive the hands-on experience necessary to build confidence and competence. They are sometimes left to watch from the sidelines, as overworked healthcare professionals struggle to provide patient care amidst resource limitations, leaving little time for the teaching and mentorship that's so crucial during clinical training.

The faltering support for doctors extends into their internship years, a critical period meant for honing practical skills. Intern doctors are often posted to hospitals where they're expected to work miracles without the requisite support or supervision. These conditions not only impact the immediate quality of healthcare but also shape the skill set and clinical judgement of the doctors that are churned out into the healthcare system.

Upon completion of internship and mandatory national service, young doctors find themselves at a crossroads. Continuing their medical education with a residency is the next logical step; however, securing a residency position is akin to engaging in a gladiatorial contest. There are far fewer residency slots than there are applicants - a situation that leaves many qualified doctors in a professional limbo, year after year.

The residency training itself, for those lucky enough to secure it, is another odyssey. It is both a time of intensive learning and an endurance test, underscored by an often capricious funding situation. The trainings are incessantly disrupted by industrial actions due to irregularities in salary payments or poor working conditions, leaving resident doctors and their patients hanging in a balance of uncertainty.

This relentless cycle is further exacerbated by the lack of specialty and sub-specialty training options within the country. Doctors interested in pursuing niche areas of medicine may have no other choice but to seek opportunities abroad. This, combined with delayed salaries and an unsupportive work environment, contributes to the brain drain that is depleting Nigeria's healthcare system of its finest minds.

For female doctors, the hurdles magnify. Balancing rigorous training schedules with societal expectations of marriage and motherhood can be particularly challenging. Maternity leaves are minimal, and returning to work often comes with its own set of prejudices and logistical nightmares, further complicating their professional trajectories.

Let's not forget the psychological toll these conditions take on the doctors in training. They often work under the shadow of mental health issues, with depression, anxiety, and burnout being common, yet there's a stark absence of robust support systems to address these concerns. The culture within the medical community often stigmatizes acknowledging such struggles, leaving many to suffer in silence.

Despite these realities, there are occasional glimmers of resilience. Some medical schools and teaching hospitals have initiated reforms by integrating novel teaching methods, facilitating research opportunities, and building partnerships with international institutions. Yet, for these to have any meaningful impact, they need to become widespread practices rather than isolated instances of progress.

In confronting these challenges, it is crucial to appreciate that the training and support of doctors is foundational to the strength and efficacy of the healthcare system as a whole. Reinvigorating these support systems requires a multilayered approach, involving government investment, educational reforms, international collaboration, and an overhaul of institutional attitudes toward healthcare education.

As we journey through the lives and livelihoods of Nigerian doctors, their valor amidst adversities deserves reverence. However, acknowledging their courage must be matched with action. Empowering the nation's caregivers with robust training and support mechanisms isn't just a moral imperative - it's a necessary investment in the health and well-being of the nation's population at large.

The Financial Pulse: Understanding Doctors' Salaries

Within the framework of the Nigerian healthcare system, the financial realities faced by its doctors are sobering. From the sprawling urban centers to the rural clinics, the incomes of Nigerian medical professionals tell a tale of inequity and hardship. Doctors, who have undergone extensive and costly training, find themselves at the mercy of a remuneration scale that falls dismally short when measured against the international yardstick. To put it simply, despite the pivotal roles they play, many of these practitioners earn less than their peers in other nations and often less than workers in less critical roles closer to home. This financial strain isn't just of personal concern for these individuals; it reverberates through the corridors of hospitals, affecting both morale and the quality of patient care. As we peel back the curtain on the earnings of Nigerian doctors, a broader understanding emerges of the sacrifices they make and the systemic issues that prompt their financial pulse to dangerously flutter, often leading to an exodus in search of more sustainable shores.

Comparative Analysis: Nigerian vs. International Pay Standards

It's an unspoken truth that any examination of the global healthcare landscape reveals stark disparities. However, the gulf in pay standards between Nigerian doctors and their international counterparts isn't just a point of contention—it's a gaping chasm that speaks volumes about the state of healthcare in the country. On the surface, it might look like a simple financial comparison, but beneath it lie complex issues of respect, resource allocation, and the perceived value of healthcare professionals.

In Nigeria, the reality for many doctors is defined more by what they lack than what they possess. While their peers in developed countries often enjoy competitive salaries, bolstered by comprehensive benefits, the situation in Nigeria is starkly different. Here, a doctor's salary barely scratches the surface of 'competitive'. The monthly take-home pay for a Nigerian medical doctor is abysmally low when considering the cost of living and the intensity of their work.

But what do these numbers look like in practical terms? A fresh medical graduate in Nigeria might earn as little as $300 a month, a figure that pales in comparison to the thousands that a counterpart in the United States or the United Kingdom might take home. Moreover, these international peers would also typically receive health insurance, paid leave, and pension plans—benefits that are often either insufficient or nonexistent for Nigerian doctors.

Factors such as currency value and the cost of living do impact direct comparisons but even considering these, Nigerian doctors' salaries are not commensurate with their workload or the critical nature of their jobs. Work environment plays a crucial role as well. In countries like Canada, for example, doctors work with state-of-the-art technology in well-maintained facilities, whereas in Nigeria, many are forced to make do with outdated equipment in hospitals where even basic utilities are unreliable.

But it's not just about the money. Job satisfaction in Nigeria is further compromised by a lack of professional development opportunities, a crucial aspect that places them behind their global peers. While a doctor in Germany or Australia might enjoy regular training and the chance to attend international conferences, Nigerian doctors are often left scrabbling for opportunities to advance their skills and knowledge, inevitably impacting their career growth.

Profit might not be the main motivation for many in the medical profession, but everyone has bills to pay, mouths to feed. The financial strain can be a silent tormentor to a doctor in Nigeria. It becomes challenging to maintain a decent standard of living, let alone invest in ongoing professional development or save for the future.

While the narrative is mostly bleak, not all Nigerian doctors languish at the bottom of the pay scale. Those who ascend to positions such as consultants may indeed command better salaries, but even these figures are not globally competitive. Plus, such positions are limited, and reaching them involves navigating a treacherous landscape of inadequate opportunities and political maneuvering. The fight to climb the professional ladder can be exhausting and is certainly not afforded to all.

The disparities have far-reaching consequences. A demoralized workforce will struggle to provide quality care. There's an undeniable connection between how much a society values its doctors and the quality of healthcare it can expect to receive. This is not merely about wages—it's also about investment in the healthcare sector, a commitment to building a sustainable system that cares for both patients and providers.

The international comparison also highlights an uncomfortable truth: unlike in Nigeria, many countries regard healthcare as a priority, and this is reflected in their investment in human resources. This difference isn't only seen in the west. Even in countries like South Africa or India, which face their own healthcare challenges, doctors earn substantially more, integration with the international medical community is stronger, and opportunities for career progression are clearer and more attainable.

As the world becomes more interconnected, the standards of healthcare globally seem to be on converging paths, yet the professionals behind the services are being left behind in some regions. The stark reality is that a Nigerian doctor's salary does not reflect the global appreciation for medical professionals, nor does it support the actual cost of living and personal sacrifice that comes with the job.

The financial divide between Nigerian and international doctors is just a symptom; the disease is the systemic undervaluation of medical professionals within the country. Nigerian doctors face a paradox: they are both lifesavers and yet, from a financial standpoint, significantly undervalued. Money isn't the sole motivator, but it is a crucial aspect of maintaining morale, quality of life, and the pursuit of professional excellence.

It's important to note that this is not an issue merely of national shame, it's a global concern. As healthcare crises like pandemics remind us, the health of one nation can impact the entire world. The undervaluation of Nigerian doctors poses a risk not just to their own country's healthcare system but also presents a potential threat to global health, as the migration of disillusioned healthcare workers leaves vulnerable populations even more exposed.

Addressing the pay gap, therefore, is not just about fairness or equity; it's about global health security. It's about recognizing that in a world where diseases do not respect borders, the hands that heal must be supported, encouraged, and adequately compensated, no matter where they choose to work.

Amidst these sobering reflections, there's hope for change. The resiliency of Nigerian doctors is testament to their commitment to healing and caring for their communities. But this is a call—a call to action for the enhancement of the Nigerian healthcare system beginning with a sincere appraisal and upliftment of the physicians' remuneration. It's a necessary step towards the acknowledgment of their skill, dedication, and profound importance to the fabric of society.

As we close this comparative chapter, we are left with a stark choice. We can continue to accept the status quo, with its erosion of medical talent and compromised patient care, or we can strive for a system that truly values its healthcare providers. For the wellbeing of Nigeria—and indeed the world—the choice must be clear.

Chapter 3:
The Exodus of Medical Talent

A s we delve deeper into the crisis plaguing the Nigerian healthcare system, we turn our focus to a particularly distressing phenomenon: the steady stream of medical professionals leaving the country. Nigerian healthcare workers, specifically doctors trained to address the unique health challenges of their country, are exiting in droves. Lured by the promise of better pay, improved working conditions, and greater opportunities for advancement, these skilled practitioners are setting their sights on foreign shores. This departure of talent leaves a gaping wound in the fabric of Nigeria's medical infrastructure, exacerbating an already dire situation. Their absence is felt deeply across communities, impacting not only those seeking care but also the morale of the health professionals who choose to remain behind. As this chapter unfolds, we confront the stark realities of a healthcare system hemorrhaging its most valuable resource—its people—and the multifaceted repercussions of this loss.

Push Factors: Why Doctors Leave Nigeria

The migration of Nigerian doctors abroad, a scenario that seems to increasingly pervade the landscape of healthcare in the country, cannot be overemphasized. This section unravels the complexity of the exodus and sheds light on the pressing reasons behind this phenomenon.

At the heart of this issue, salaries stand out. The financial remuneration for Nigerian medical practitioners is dire when compared to their counterparts in more affluent countries. The promise of better pay abroad is a resounding call to which many Nigerian doctors have heeded. This disparity is not just in basic salaries but extends to hazard allowances, pensions, and other benefits that are often either lacking or minuscule for those that toil in Nigeria's hospitals and clinics.

Besides financial incentives, the pursuit of a higher quality of life is also a strong motivating force. Frequent power outages, poor water supply, and substandard living conditions are daily realities that many professionals aim to transcend. The comparative comfort and stability found elsewhere offer a compelling argument for relocation.

Infrastructure challenges in the Nigerian health sector also push doctors away. Many healthcare facilities are in a state of disrepair, lacking basic equipment and technology necessary for effective medical care. This not only hampers the doctors' ability to practice but also puts patients at risk, a situation that weighs heavily on medical professionals who solemnly swore to do no harm.

The education and career growth prospects in Nigeria often pale in comparison to opportunities available abroad. Continuous professional development is stymied by the scarcity of resources and training programs. Doctors looking to specialize or pursue further education find their ambitions throttled, creating a frustration that gradually steers them towards greener pastures.

For doctors in Nigeria, the work environment can be demanding and hostile. High patient-to-doctor ratios result in burnout and stress due to overwork. These professionals face immense pressure and are often expected to perform miracles without the necessary support or resources, leading many to seek work environments abroad where they can practice more sustainably.

Inadequate healthcare policies and poor governance also play a significant role. Bureaucratic entanglements and policy paralysis hobble the healthcare system, leading to a demoralizing work environment. The impact of corruption and mismanagement of healthcare resources further exacerbates the decay and leads to disillusionment among medical practitioners.

The social unrest and insecurity in certain parts of Nigeria further exacerbate the situation. Worries about personal and family safety, combined with the general socio-political instability, drive doctors to consider their career options outside the nation's borders.

The lack of research and innovation opportunities in Nigeria is another significant factor. Doctors passionate about advancing medical science and contributing to pioneering research find little to no infrastructure supporting such endeavors at home. The allure of well-funded, cutting-edge research facilities abroad is understandably strong.

Professional recognition and respect is a subtle yet powerful factor. In a system beleaguered by numerous challenges, doctors often find themselves underappreciated. This lack of respect can manifest in poor treatment by employers, government, and sometimes the public, all of which chips away at professional satisfaction.

Furthermore, the quality of patient care that doctors can provide in Nigeria is often compromised due to systemic inefficiencies. Many healthcare professionals yearn to operate in environments where they can actually make a significant difference, leading to better patient outcomes and professional fulfillment.

Given these daunting challenges, the decision to leave Nigeria does not come lightly to most doctors. It is born out of a desire for a better professional life where their skills can be fully utilized, and their contributions valued. They grapple with the tension between national loyalty and personal as well as professional aspirations.

Even more disruptive is the emotional toll this exodus has on the doctors' personal lives. Relocation often means separation from family, friends, and the familiar contours of one's homeland. The emotional impact can be severe, pointing to the depth of despondency that must exist to push these individuals to make such life-altering decisions.

Finally, one of the most salient yet underrecognized factors is the aspiration for better healthcare systems. Many doctors leave with the hope that by gaining experience abroad, they can eventually contribute to improving Nigeria's healthcare system, whether through diaspora networks, remittances, or knowledge transfer upon their return.

The combination of these factors creates a potent force driving Nigerian doctors to leave their home country. As they exit, they carry with them the hope for change, the pain of separation, and the aspiration that one day, the tide will turn in favor of an improved Nigerian healthcare system that can retain its much-needed medical talent.

The Impact on Nigerian Healthcare Systems

The Nigerian healthcare system stands at a critical juncture, grappling with a mass exodus of medical professionals that threatens the very foundation of patient care across the nation. This brain drain has far-reaching consequences, echoing through cramped urban hospitals and echoing even louder in the scant clinics of rural areas. At the heart of the issue are Nigerian doctors, trained within the country's medical schools, who find themselves compelled to seek greener pastures overseas.

Physicians, the bedrock of any healthcare system, are leaving in droves, driven away by substandard working conditions and seeking the allure of better compensation abroad. Each departure not only signifies a loss of investment in training and expertise but also stretches the remaining medical workforce even thinner, exacerbating an already perilous patient-to-doctor ratio.

In hospitals where a single doctor once juggled the workload of managing outpatient services, inpatient wards, and emergency responses, now the remaining few must bear this burden alone. The consequences are palpable – longer wait times for patients, truncated consultations, and a creeping fatigue that shadows these committed professionals, heightening the risk of burnout and medical errors.

Rural healthcare, more fragile due to its isolation and resource scarcity, suffers disproportionately from this talent hemorrhage. With fewer specialists available, conditions that could be managed or cured with timely intervention often escalate into life-threatening emergencies. The promise of universal healthcare coverage remains a distant dream for many as the reality of inaccessible and inadequate care looms large.

Nigeria's public health initiatives, designed to combat infectious diseases and improve maternal and child health, find themselves undercut by the shortage of healthcare providers. Immunization campaigns and preventive healthcare services, which rely on skilled personnel at their helm, face disruption, creating openings for disease outbreaks that could have otherwise been prevented.

Training institutions, such as teaching hospitals and medical colleges, are not immune to the fallout. Their faculty numbers dwindle, and with that, the capacity to train the next generation of medical practitioners wanes. The mentorship essential for developing highly skilled physicians can't keep pace, compromising the quality of education and future care standards.

The salary disparities between Nigerian doctors and their international counterparts have led to a situation where investment in medical education often translates to a loss for the nation. A doctor's decision to migrate is not merely professional but has a societal cost, impacting the health sector's sustainability and Nigeria's developmental trajectory.

Emergency medical response systems, already erratic due to infrastructural insufficiencies, are further destabilized without sufficient medical professionals. The golden hour—the critical period where prompt medical attention can save lives—is all too often squandered, not for lack of will, but for the absence of hands ready to provide the necessary care.

Specialist care suffers a similar fate, as niche fields like oncology, cardiology, and neurology see their talent pool evaporate. Patients in need of specialized treatment are frequently left with no choice but to join the increasing number seeking medical treatment abroad, incurring exorbitant costs and logistical challenges.

The government's role in mitigating this trend is vital but currently falls short. Policies intended to retain healthcare talent are too often marred by delays or insufficient incentives. The loss of medical professionals undermines not just current health delivery but the government's capacity to respond to future health crises. Without sufficient talent at home, response efforts become sluggish and inefficient.

Non-Governmental Organizations (NGOs) working within the Nigerian healthcare space encounter additional obstacles due to the shortage of trained medical professionals. Their efforts to improve health outcomes and infrastructure are hindered, demanding an increased reliance on foreign medical volunteers, which is neither sustainable nor empowering for local systems in the long term.

The Nigerian healthcare system's resilience is continuously tested, reliant on the dedication of those who remain to provide care amid adversity. Nevertheless, it can't be ignored that each physician who leaves not only diminishes the system's strength but also conveys a powerful message about the country's inability to retain its brightest minds.

Efforts to implement technology in healthcare also suffer in the absence of adequately trained personnel to operate and maintain these systems. Digital health initiatives, telemedicine, and electronic health records are crucial elements for progression, but they require consistent professional expertise which is currently haemorrhaging out of the country.

It can be hard to find silver linings in such a situation, but the diaspora of Nigerian medical professionals does have potential benefits—remittances sent back home and the establishment of international networks that can be leveraged for knowledge and technology transfer. However, these benefits pale in comparison to the vast needs of a population that continues to face an under-resourced and over-stretched healthcare system.

Ultimately, the exodus of medical talent from Nigeria creates a cyclical strain: as the system deteriorates, more doctors leave, and this exodus further degrades the system. Breaking this cycle demands not just strong policy responses, but also a collective will to invest in the healthcare system—ensuring that it's equipped to care for the nation's people and retain the valuable physicians trained to heal them.

Chapter 4:
The Illusion of Accessible Healthcare

The term 'accessible healthcare' casts a promising glow on the notion that services are readily available to all who need them. Yet, for millions in Nigeria, this is a mirage that crumbles under scrutiny. Cloaked beneath this guise of availability is a labyrinthine tale of disparities so stark that one's geographic location can be the arbiter of life or death. Urban centers, with their bustling clinics and hospitals, paint a deceiving picture of efficiency, while rural areas languish in neglect, their cries for help often lost in the void. This chapter exposes the chasm between the haves and the have-nots, highlighting the grim reality that, while healthcare may exist, it is a specter out of reach for the poorest and most vulnerable. The illusion shatters further when considering the wallet-emptying expenses that come unannounced, wielding financial ruin for families already teetering on the edge of economic despair. Narratives of hollow promises and extinguished hopes run rampant, a chorus of voices underscoring the need for a system that truly embodies the ethos of care for everyone.

Urban vs. Rural Disparities

In the quest for equitable healthcare in Nigeria, there is a persistent and troubling disparity between urban and rural areas. While gleaming hospitals and clinics may dot the landscape of major cities, rural regions languish with inadequacies in facilities, healthcare professionals, and basic medical services. This divide not only undermines the concept of accessible healthcare but also reflects a deeper issue of uneven development and the neglect of rural populations.

The illusion of accessible healthcare is most starkly broken when examining the infrastructure in rural areas. In many villages, primary healthcare centers, if they exist at all, are often dilapidated and lacking basics such as running water or reliable electricity. Contrast that with urban areas, which may have private clinics boasting state-of-the-art equipment, and the inequality is palpable. Understanding this dichotomy requires scrutiny of more than buildings and facilities; it demands a look at the availability of human resources.

Doctors in Nigeria face a tough choice between staying in rural areas, where their services are sorely needed, or migrating to urban centers or abroad, where pay and working conditions are significantly better. The salaries of doctors in rural regions are frequently not commensurate with the hardships they bear, such as isolation, lack of professional support, and sometimes an increased workload due to the scarcity of healthcare workers. What's more, the financial incentives and opportunities for professional development that do exist are often centered in cities, further luring doctors away from rural practices.

When considering the staffing of medical facilities, one finds a glaring shortage of professionals in the countryside. There are untold stories of rural clinics manned by a single doctor—or none at all—forcing nurses and midwives to perform duties that exceed their training. In urban hospitals, meanwhile, a patient might choose from a variety of specialists. This urban-rural divide not only restricts access to healthcare for rural dwellers but also can lead to worse health outcomes.

A look into maternal health services further illustrates these disparities. In rural areas, expecting mothers might need to travel long distances on rough roads to access prenatal care; a journey that is often dangerous and unaffordable. As a result, home births without skilled attendants are common, leading to higher rates of maternal and infant mortality. In contrast, urban mothers usually have many hospitals and specialized health centers from which to choose.

The dearth of medical equipment in rural areas cannot be overstated. Diagnostic tools such as ultrasound machines, blood analysis kits, and even basic medications can be scarce, while urban hospitals might struggle with the capacity to service their equipment due to the high turn-around. This disparity in diagnostic and treatment capabilities contributes to a healthcare system that is imbalanced and inefficient.

It's imperative to acknowledge the psychological toll these disparities have on healthcare providers. For those in rural areas facing overwhelming need and insufficient resources, burnout and disillusionment are common. These feelings are compounded by the knowledge that their urban counterparts have access to better resources and often more manageable workloads—an understanding that eats away at one's dedication to service.

Quality healthcare in rural communities is further imperiled by the challenges of health education and awareness. Urban residents generally have greater access to information on preventive measures, health campaigns, and awareness programs. In contrast, rural populations are often left out of such conversations, leading to a lack of understanding of healthy practices and therefore a higher risk of preventable diseases.

In emergencies, the contrast between urban and rural provision becomes a life-or-death matter. Urban dwellers may count on ambulance services and emergency care that is readily available; meanwhile, in rural settings, the dearth of immediate care can turn treatable conditions into fatal ones. The importance of prompt medical attention in such cases cannot be overstressed, yet for many in rural Nigeria, it remains a distant dream.

Children in rural areas are also disadvantaged when it comes to healthcare. From immunizations to treatment for common childhood illnesses, healthcare services are frequently out of reach. Urban children, on the other hand, benefit from regular vaccination programs and pediatric care, which are critical to their development and overall wellbeing.

Nonetheless, this divide is seen not only in health services but in health outcomes. There is a higher prevalence of certain diseases in rural populations, as they lack the basic infrastructure to manage conditions such as waterborne illnesses, malnutrition, and infectious diseases, which are less prevalent in urban centers due to better living conditions and access to healthcare.

Patients themselves face a multitude of challenges in rural areas. Besides the obvious difficulty in accessing healthcare, the costs associated with travel, lost work, and sometimes the need to pay out-of-pocket for services that are supposedly free, make healthcare unattainable for many. Despite the existence of national health insurance schemes, the reality on the ground often does not match policy pronouncements, especially in rural regions.

The prognosis for addressing urban-rural disparities in Nigerian healthcare requires innovative interventions and substantial investments. It's apparent that merely constructing more clinics is not enough. There must be concerted efforts to retain and support healthcare workers in rural areas, such as through enhanced salaries, benefits, and opportunities for continuous education that are on par with those offered in urban centers.

Telemedicine, mobile health units, and community health worker programs could serve as vital lifelines, connecting rural populations with the healthcare ecosystem. Moreover, tapping into renewable energy sources could solve some of the infrastructure problems plaguing these areas, ensuring that when doctors and equipment are available, they can be used effectively.

In summary, this urban-rural healthcare chasm reinforces the illusion of universal healthcare access in Nigeria, a mirage fading away under the harsh light of reality. The cost of this disparity is measured not just in naira and kobos but in lives—the ultimate price for a nation's collective failure to ensure that healthcare truly becomes a right, not a privilege dictated by geography.

In the following chapters, we will delve deeper into particular facets of this vast and complex issue, examining the implications of overburdened healthcare workers on patient care, the potential for technological remedies, and the gripping personal experiences of those practicing medicine in Nigeria today.

Hidden Costs for Patients

While Nigeria proclaims healthcare accessibility, an iceberg of hidden costs lurks beneath the surface, threatening the financial stability of its citizens. High medical bills are just the tip of the iceberg; for many, indirect expenses associated with receiving healthcare can be crippling. Transport, lost income during hospital visits, and the purchase of basic medical supplies—these are the burdens shouldered by the Nigerian patient.

Consider the rural villager, faced with the daunting journey to an urban hospital. The distances are not trivial—often they span hundreds of kilometers. The cost of transportation can quickly add up to more than the typical rural worker earns in several weeks. And for a healthcare system already struggling, there's rarely an ambulance or subsidized transit in sight.

Emergencies and long-term treatments compound these costs exponentially. Every trip to a hospital or clinic is a day's wages forfeited for many. Those with chronic illnesses or conditions requiring regular medical attention find themselves in debilitating cycles of debt and disease. The absence from work strips away not just their earnings, but sometimes leads to job loss—a price far too high for seeking health.

Adding to the financial stress, the shortage of medical supplies in many Nigerian facilities means that patients must procure their own. Gloves, syringes, even bed linens—items that should be standard in healthcare environments—become out-of-pocket expenses. This practice not only drains the patient's resources but also raises the risk of infection and complications from unsterile or inadequate supplies.

The emotional toll of these hidden costs is as significant as the financial one. The sick must navigate a terrain of uncertainty and anxiety, negotiating prices at every turn, never sure if they can afford the next necessary step in their treatment. The mental strain can impede recovery, or worse, dissuade individuals from seeking care at the onset of illness.

Catastrophic health expenses—costs that exceed a particular threshold of a family's income—are a grim reality for many Nigerians. A single health incident can wipe out savings, plunge families into poverty, and perpetuate the cycle of hardship. Healthcare, a beacon of hope, transforms into a potential financial disaster.

The ripple effects touch education and nutrition as well. Families forced to direct funds to medical care divert monetary resources from school fees and food. Children's futures are mortgaged for the sake of present emergencies. The repercussions echo well into the future, compromising education and well-being.

Women, often the primary caregivers, bear a disproportionate brunt of these hidden costs. They must negotiate the caretaking of their sick family members while managing the home and sometimes working multiple jobs. The opportunity costs for them are monumental, limiting their potential and their contribution to economic development.

Insurance schemes, where available, offer scant relief. Coverage is limited, and the bureaucracy is labyrinthine. Many find the process of claims so daunting or delayed that they resort to paying out of pocket regardless of their policy. The promise of insurance thus fails to materialize into tangible assistance for countless Nigerians.

Unforeseen costs cut across every socio-economic class, but those living in poverty feel it most acutely. A wealthy individual might negotiate the inefficiencies of the healthcare system with money and influence, but the poor are left to the mercy of an inaccessible framework that amplifies their hardships.

Even basic medical procedures become luxuries beyond reach. A simple appendectomy can result in a financial upheaval from which recovery is as challenging as from the surgery itself. The social injustice inherent in such a system is stark; one's health should not be dictated by wealth, but in Nigeria, it often is.

There is an urgent need for a scalable solution that protects the vulnerable from these predatory costs. Subsidies, robust insurance plans, and genuine reform are not optional but essential. Without it, the very fabric of Nigerian society is at risk, with the poor and sick facing the most significant peril.

By shedding light on these hidden costs, we identify a crucial aspect of healthcare reform. Acknowledgment is merely the first step; action must follow. Only when the full spectrum of costs is considered can healthcare in Nigeria move towards the equitable and accessible ideal it posits to embody.

In conclusion, the hidden costs represent a stark contradiction to the notion of accessible healthcare. They are an anathema to the principles of universal and equitable healthcare, encapsulated in the Sustainable Development Goals. It is incumbent upon us all—policymakers, healthcare providers, and society—to confront this reality and work tirelessly towards a system where health does not become a harbinger of financial ruin.

Indeed, as we chart the course of Nigerian healthcare, these hidden costs must be brought to the fore. They tell a story of a nation at a critical juncture—one where the path to wellness is fraught with obstacles, financial and otherwise, that only concerted effort and compassionate policy can address. It is the reality for countless Nigerians, and it is a reality we can no longer afford to ignore.

Chapter 5:
Stretched Thin: The Patient-to-Doctor Ratio

Imagine walking into a clinic with the hope of immediate medical attention, only to be met with a sea of waiting patients and a palpably exhausted medical staff fighting a losing battle against the clock. This chapter peels back the layers of the stark reality facing Nigeria's healthcare system, where the patient-to-doctor ratio stretches beyond the breaking point. In Nigeria, the number of doctors is woefully insufficient, and the ramifications are far-reaching. There is a complex interplay here: a frayed workforce translates into rushed consultations, misdiagnoses, and often a complete lack of follow-up care—outcomes that are unacceptable in any patient's book. The scarcity of healthcare professionals also means preventable diseases gain a stronghold, chronic conditions go unmanaged, and the progress to reduce mortality rates is bitterly slow. These are not mere statistics; we're talking about people's lives hanging in the balance. As the evidence mounts, it becomes starkly clear that the implications of such skewed healthcare dynamics ripple outward, eroding the fabric of society as a whole and leaving individuals, families, and communities vulnerable in its wake.

The Overburdened Workforce

Within the strained corridors of Nigerian hospitals, the workforce bears a weight that bends resilience to its limits. Doctors who've endured years of rigorous training find themselves facing relentless torrents of patients, with numbers vastly disproportional to the hands available for care. Such extreme patient-to-doctor ratios result not only in exhaustion but also raise concerns about the quality of care being compromised. As they navigate an underfunded system with one of the lowest healthcare budgets in the world, these physicians grapple with salaries that scarcely reflect their critical roles or the intensity of their labor. The grinding gears of this overstretched ecosystem churn more than just numbers; they grind down the very spirit and capability of a workforce expected to perform medical miracles against all odds. Yet, despite these challenges, Nigerian doctors show a commendable level of dedication, underscoring a stark contrast between the value of their work and the compensation that greets their efforts.

Consequences for Patient Care Within the straining confines of the Nigerian healthcare system, the quality of patient care has been compromised. The patient-to-doctor ratio in Nigeria tells a story of inadequacy and overburdened medical professionals. With an increasing population, the demand for healthcare is surging, pressing against a system plagued by shortages and the exodus of qualified personnel.

Consider the grueling hours that Nigerian doctors work under intense pressure, servicing far more patients than is advised by international healthcare standards. These medical professionals routinely encounter the reality of under-resourced and overcrowded hospitals. The direct fallout of these conditions is a healthcare service that is stretched thin, often unable to meet the needs of its patients efficiently or safely.

The situation precipitates a variety of consequential outcomes; one of the most visible is lengthy wait times for patients. Those in need of urgent care may find themselves caught in an indeterminable waiting game, as doctors juggle a multitude of cases. Time-sensitive treatments get delayed, opportunities for early intervention are missed, and conditions that could have been managed with prompt medical attention spiral into complex health crises.

A significant indirect repercussion of the high patient-to-doctor ratio is the reduced time doctors can afford to each individual patient. The cultivation of doctor-patient relationships, crucial in the effective management of chronic diseases and long-term care, is hampered. This situation not only detracts from the quality of care but also from the satisfaction and trust patients have in their healthcare providers.

Adding to the distress, the overburdened doctors often experience burnout. The perpetual state of workload excess creates undue stress and can lead to a decrease in performance and attention, which, in the gravest scenarios, may result in medical errors—a matter of serious concern in patient safety.

There's also the sobering reality of diagnostics and treatment plans. The constraint of resources often means that the diagnostics are not as comprehensive as they could be. Doctors, in their bid to manage the limited resources, might resort to empirical treatments rather than evidence-based medicine. The implication of this practice is particularly dire for conditions such as cancers, where early and accurate diagnosis holds critical importance.

Similarly, truncated patient encounters may lead doctors to miss or dismiss subtle symptoms, compounding the likelihood of misdiagnosis. A patient's health narrative is nuanced, and a rushed consultation can lead to oversights. This is true for ailments with complex presentations or where cultural factors influence the perception and articulation of symptoms.

Inadequate doctor compensation further exacerbates the quality of patient care. When financial remuneration fails to reflect the intensity and necessity of the service doctors provide, morale dips; a dispirited healthcare provider is less likely to deliver care with the compassion and diligence required. Not to mention, the financial strain might push doctors to seek additional income sources, detracting further from their focus and energy on patient care.

The attrition of doctors to foreign shores, in search of better opportunities, bespeaks a significant brain drain that is stripping Nigerian hospitals of their most experienced clinicians. This loss goes beyond numbers; experience and mentorship are critical in nurturing a robust healthcare workforce, shaping the competencies and confidence of junior doctors, and maintaining a standard of care that patients desperately need.

Crucial too is the impact on medical training and education within the nation. With fewer experienced doctors to serve as tutors and mentors, the training of medical students and residents is compromised. This phenomenon raises serious concerns about the future standard of healthcare, patient care, and the sustainability of the healthcare system as a whole.

In rural areas, the impact is even more pronounced. The scant availability of healthcare professionals in these regions means that residents are often reliant on under-trained health workers for primary care. This reliance can lead to a disconnect in the understanding and treatment of more complex or non-communicable diseases, widening the health gap between the urban and rural populations.

Emergencies expose another gaping wound in the patient care system. The healthcare infrastructure in many parts is unable to support effective emergency care. With insufficient emergency departments and a lack of trained staff, life-saving interventions are not prompt, exacerbating mortality rates from conditions that could otherwise be managed.

It's worth noting that the consequences on patient care contribute to a larger narrative. The shortcomings in the healthcare system detrimentally affect not only individual health but collective productivity. A population plagued by untreated or poorly managed health conditions faces challenges in maintaining educational goals and economic participation.

The ripples of inadequate patient care reflect in societal attitudes. Distrust and dissatisfaction towards the healthcare system can lead individuals to delay seeking medical help or to turn to alternative and sometimes unsafe practices. This further entrenches the cycle of ill-health and underlines the gravity of attending to the healthcare system's flaws.

Finally, the consequence of retaining doctors through adequate salaries, support, and working conditions cannot be overstated. It is paramount to not only address the symptoms but the systemic issues causing these symptoms. A stronger foundation will provide sustainable patient care improvements, ultimately leading to a healthier population and a more robust Nigerian society.

Chapter 6:
Policy Paralysis and Bureaucratic Ailments

Navigating the complexities of Nigeria's healthcare policy labyrinth reveals a harrowing tale of stagnation and inefficiency. At the crux of the matter lies policy paralysis—a crippling inability to enact and enforce meaningful reforms that address the dire straits of the healthcare system. Entrenched bureaucratic ailments further exacerbate this inertia. While government entities grapple with their responsibilities to safeguard public health, a detailed dissection exposes persistent veins of corruption and mismanagement within health sectors. These pathological governance issues not only thwart initiatives for improvement but also breed a chronic distrust among those dependent on the system's revival. This chapter delves into the murky waters of administrative dysfunction, untangling the web of failures that hamper progress and perpetuate the suffering of both patients and practitioners in a cycle that seems to defy resolution.

Government Responsibilities and Failings

As we examine the landscape of Nigeria's healthcare system, one cannot overlook the government's pivotal role and its inability, at times, to live up to the responsibilities entrusted to it. This regrettable oversight has far-reaching consequences for both healthcare practitioners and patients alike. The government of Nigeria bears the weight of ensuring accessible, quality healthcare for its populace—a weight that, unfortunately, appears too often unshouldered.

When it comes to the governance of healthcare systems, the federal and state governments have a binding duty to set beneficial policies, regulate standards, and allocate sufficient funds. In Nigeria, however, we see a gaping disconnect between policy formulation and implementation. The policies may be articulate on paper, but the translation into tangible health benefits for citizens is frustratingly missing.

The allocation of funds for healthcare in Nigeria raises unending questions. Despite repeated calls from global health bodies, Nigeria's allocation to healthcare remains critically low, a clear neglect of the Abuja Declaration which stipulates that at least 15% of the national budget should be dedicated to health. This shortfall translates into alarming deficits in infrastructure, resources, and manpower.

Nigeria's medical professionals wade through the mire of bureaucratic red tape daily. Systems intended to aid their work have turned into barriers. Doctors' salaries, as a point in case, are dogged by delays and discrepancies, causing low morale and propelling many to seek greener pastures. A government's failure to pay its doctors competitive, timely wages not only displays a lack of acknowledgment for their vital service but also undermines the stability of the entire healthcare sector.

The impacts, both immediate and collateral, of these governmental failings are felt on the ground level. Overburdened facilities and a dearth of critical supplies mean patients battle for attention in crowded wards. Reports of patients being asked to purchase basic supplies such as gloves or syringes are symptomatic of these systemic deficiencies. It's a cruel irony when sick individuals, in their most vulnerable state, are compelled to navigate additional roadblocks instead of receiving prompt healthcare interventions.

The evolution of any healthcare system is contingent upon its ability to integrate research and feedback for continuous improvement. However, in Nigeria, there's a pronounced lag in updating practice protocols to align with current research, due largely to bureaucratic sluggishness. This failure to evolve not only diminishes the quality of care but also contributes to the brain drain of medical professionals seeking environments where their skills are both up-to-date and valued.

Despite the noteworthy efforts of NGOs and international agencies, their work cannot supplant the government's role. A coordinated approach that goes beyond piecemeal fixes toward sustainable solutions is required, and it starts with government initiative and accountability.

Transparency, a principle often heralded yet seldom realized, is an antidote to mismanagement and corruption that plague the healthcare system. The opacity of operations and financial dealings within the health ministry and its parastatals casts a shadow over their credibility. This dimming faith in the system not only discourages investment but also hinders concerted efforts at reform.

The deficit of trust between healthcare professionals and the government is a chasm that has widened over time. Recurring industrial actions by medical professionals underscore the depth of discontent and the urgency of redress. It's both a symptom of systemic illness and a call to action—a call that demands more than ad hoc remediation.

The modicum of healthcare services available to the rural populace further illustrates governmental neglect. The urban-rural divide in healthcare delivery is a stark reality, with disparities in accessibility and quality widening that chasm. If the government does not uphold its mandate to serve all of its citizens, including those in the most remote corners, it is failing in one of its most fundamental obligations.

In analyzing the series of challenges that beleaguer Nigeria's healthcare system, one can't help but arrive at a disconcerting conclusion: that the Nigerian government has, through acts of omission or commission, faltered in fulfilling its roles. This failure is insidious, eroding the foundation of healthcare delivery and casting a long shadow over the prospects of an ailing population.

But despair is not our destination. There is room for redemption, albeit through substantial and systemic change. The government of Nigeria must revitalize its approaches, prioritize healthcare, and actualize policies with resolute action. Lives depend on this crucial pivot, and the healthcare system's sustainability hinges on the government's responsiveness to its failings.

Protestations and promises will not bandage the wounds inflicted by governmental neglect. Concrete measures, fortified with the mortar of political will and civic duty, are the only means to rebuild. Listening to healthcare professionals, investing in training, and ensuring fair compensation are steps that cannot be delayed. Indeed, installing a robust framework for transparency and accountability is imperative for restoring trust within the system.

Signs of hope are not absent in this critique. Instances of exceptional governance do exist, but these bright spots are too infrequent and frayed to stitch together a complete remedy. What is needed is a consistent, nationwide commitment to valuing and nurturing the Nigerian healthcare system—all hands must be on deck, with the government at the helm, steering toward calmer, healthier waters.

As we move towards the succeeding chapters, the strain put forth by the lingering policy paralysis and bureaucratic ailments will come under further scrutiny. The focus will shift to narrower alleyways, yet all rooted in the fertile ground of governmental responsibility—or the lack thereof. It's in these trenches where the fight for a more resilient Nigerian healthcare system will be won or lost.

Corruption and Mismanagement in Health Sectors

In the intricately woven fabric of Nigerian healthcare, threads of corruption and managerial inadequacy have caused significant detriment to the provision of quality medical services. The labyrinthine bureaucracy that ensnares hospitals and clinics across Nigeria is not just a procedural nuisance, but a veritable wilting of the system from within.

While the Nigerian government has pledged time and again to improve healthcare delivery, these promises are often adulterated by corruption at various administrative levels. Funds allocated for healthcare development have been found diverted, lined into pockets of unscrupulous officials rather than reaching the clinics for which they were intended. This pilfering of resources lays bare a stark reality: the denuding of funds earmarks a gross misallocation, loading the dice against positive patient outcomes.

The mismanagement that plagues the health sectors can take on many forms. Often, it manifests in hiring practices, where nepotism reigns supreme over meritocracy. Hospitals, in dire need of skilled practitioners, instead find their ranks stuffed with underqualified appointees who wield connections as their primary skill. This practice not only undercuts the morale of diligent healthcare professionals but also compromises the care that patients receive.

Beyond hiring, administrative disarray also hobbles procurement processes. Rather than adorning hospitals with state-of-the-art equipment, one discovers a bizarre procurement of outdated or even non-functioning apparatuses that litter the hallways of healthcare facilities—mute testimony to wasted investment and ill-considered planning.

Echoes of graft and corruption ripple through the pricing systems of medical services and supplies. Kickbacks and price inflation contort what should be a straightforward path to receiving healthcare into a gauntlet of financial exploitation for the average Nigerian. Such systems have eroded trust between patients and the healthcare establishment, with many suspecting that their health is not the priority.

The financial mismanagement extends to the remuneration of doctors, which is steeped in irregularity and delay. The palpable discontent among the nation's doctors regarding their pay—which pales in comparison to international standards—is exacerbated by the unpunctual delivery of their monthly dues. It is no wonder that the exodus of medical professionals seeking fair compensation and better working conditions has escalated to alarming levels.

Inventory control within hospitals and clinics is another casualty of mismanagement. Essential drugs and medical supplies are often found to have been misappropriated or allowed to waste away in storerooms due to sheer negligence. This compromises the healing process and places patients in jeopardy as critical treatments must be delayed or substituted with less effective measures.

Fraudulent insurance claims have also been part and parcel of a complicated web that sees the siphoning of millions designated for healthcare. Insurers, healthcare providers, and sometimes patients collude to submit false claims, draining resources that could potentially serve the health needs of many more Nigerians in need.

While these issues persist, accountability remains a hollow concept. Audits which are carried out are either sporadic or lack the teeth to bring about any substantive penalization or reform. Whistleblowers who might bring these issues to light find little in the way of protection or incentive—often facing retaliation instead of commendation.

To compound the situation, strategic planning for future healthcare contingencies is undermined by the volatile nature of these corrupt practices. The absence of consistent leadership and transparent long-term goals leaves the health sectors perpetually unstable and unprepared, particularly glaring in the face of public health challenges like the recent COVID-19 pandemic.

Data falsification has also been noted, as health administrators sometimes massage figures to present a more favorable, although misleading, picture of their performance. This dishonesty may temporarily please political superiors, but the long-term damage is to the detriment of a truthful appraisal of healthcare needs and the effective deployment of resources.

Paradoxically, the diversion of healthcare funding has inadvertently created an environment of scarcity that drives further corrupt behavior. Doctors and nurses may find themselves pressured to game the system, be it through acceptance of bribes to prioritize care or to engage in private practice while on official time.

Addressing these festering wounds requires a cumulative approach—heightening transparency, rewarding honesty, and enforcing the rule of law without prejudice. The potential of health sectors to deliver lifesaving care hangs in the balance, hinged upon the dedication to vigorously cleansing the current system of its sustained maladies.

What rings clear is that the salary woes of Nigerian doctors serve as a sober indicator of a system in distress. Their financial struggles reflect a broader narrative of dysfunction—one that must be reframed to ensure not only that they are compensated with dignity but that the very bulwark of healthcare in Nigeria is salvaged from the swamp of corruption and mismanagement.

In the broader picture, understanding the gravity of this situation is imperative for any meaningful advancement of healthcare in Nigeria. Reform is not an option; it is a necessity that begs immediate attention if the lives and well-being of millions are to be more than a footnote in the annals of policy paralysis and bureaucratic ailments.

Chapter 7:
The Technology Gap in Diagnosis and Treatment

In stark contrast to the well-equipped clinics of developed nations, the technological disparities in Nigeria's healthcare landscape paint a somber picture—one where the absence of modern diagnostic tools and treatment methods severely confines medical capabilities. Even as medical knowledge evolves at a breakneck pace globally, doctors in Nigeria face an uphill battle, struggling to offer care with outdated equipment, if any at all. The chasm between available technology and that which is needed to provide adequate healthcare services has repercussions that echo through each failed diagnosis and exacerbated illness. This chapter delves into the extent to which the shortage of cutting-edge medical technology has impeded proper patient care and outlines the ramifications of such a gap on the health outcomes of Nigeria's population. It seeks to unravel the complex tapestry of underfunding, neglect, and missed opportunities in technological adoption that has relegated an entire healthcare system to the margins of modern medical practice.

The Role of Innovation

In navigating the technological rift that characterizes the Nigerian healthcare system, innovation emerges as a key to bridging the diagnostic and treatment chasm. The potency of pioneering ideas and digital health solutions can't be understated, as they offer glimmers of hope against the backdrop of a starkly under-equipped medical landscape. Embracing telemedicine, mobile health apps, and electronic medical records could revolutionize patient care, even under the shadow of scant resources and overstretched personnel. Innovation isn't just an optional luxury; it's a critical lifeline, one that promises to elevate the quality of healthcare delivery without necessitating the steep costs that traditional improvements might incur. Moreover, such advancements illuminate a pathway to empowerment for healthcare providers, gifting them the tools to combat the deep-seated inefficiencies and systemic neglect they face daily. Agile, responsive, and resource-conscious, technological innovation is not just about adopting new gadgets—it's about rekindling resilience within Nigeria's beleaguered healthcare ecosystem.

Limitations and Hopes for the Future

As we peer into the complexities of technological advancements in the Nigerian healthcare sector, it is necessary to acknowledge the glaring limitations that currently hamper progress. The narrative of innovation in healthcare within Nigeria can't be told without recognizing that the infrastructure necessary as a foundation for these technologies is often lacking. In a landscape where electricity and internet access are uncertain, deploying sophisticated medical technology becomes a formidable challenge.

One limitation is the cost. Many hospitals and clinics struggle to afford the most basic supplies, leaving little room in the budget for technological investments. This financial constraint means that the adoption of advanced diagnostic tools and electronic health records, which are commonplace in developed countries, remain a distant dream for many Nigerian healthcare providers.

Further limiting technological progress is the educational divide. While some Nigerian doctors and medical staff are trained to use cutting-edge equipment and software, many have limited experience with such tools. The knowledge gap can lead to underutilization of the technology that is available, undermining potential improvements in patient care and operational efficiency.

Coupled with educational limitations, there's the issue of maintenance. High-tech medical devices require regular servicing, often by specialists who are in short supply. Where equipment does exist, it can become quickly obsolete when repairs and updates aren't maintained, effectively compounding issues of scarcity and obsolescence.

Moving beyond the technological quagmires, there's the barrier of bureaucratic inertia. Policy shifts and governmental support necessary to integrate technology into healthcare have been lethargic. Embracing technological solutions requires systemic changes, substantial investment, and a departure from the status quo, all of which are met with resistance at various levels of government.

Yet despite these significant hurdles, hope persists among the medical community in Nigeria. There is a burgeoning awareness within the sector that technology could be a catalyst for sweeping improvements. In some urban clinics, electronic record-keeping is slowly being implemented, bolstering capacity for data analysis that can drive better healthcare outcomes.

Telemedicine also poses an exciting avenue for expanding access to care, particularly in remote or underserved regions. With a mobile penetration rate that soars over many African countries, Nigeria has an opportunity to harness mobile technology for remote diagnosis and treatment, bypassing infrastructural deficiencies to an extent.

What's more, the rise in public-private partnerships presents potential resource pools for technological development. By collaborating with tech companies and embracing innovative funding models, the healthcare sector stands to make strides that government funding alone has not achieved.

The decentralization of healthcare services through community-based health programs has also been identified as a promising approach. This model allows for more localized management of limited resources and can lay the groundwork for the integration of technology at a community level, which is often more adaptable to change and innovation.

In the arena of education, there is an increasing push for technology to play a substantial role in medical training. By aligning medical curricula with the digital age, the next generation of healthcare professionals can be better prepared to utilize and advance healthcare technology in Nigeria.

Perhaps as important as technological advancement is the potential uptick in international collaboration. Knowledge exchange programs and funding from global health organizations could prove instrumental in breaching the tech gap, allowing Nigerian medical professionals to learn from the successes and failures of other nations.

Efforts to domesticate medical technology production have also started to materialize. Recognizing the impracticality of reliance on imports, there's a burgeoning interest in nurturing a local medical technology industry. By nurturing tech startups and encouraging local innovation, Nigeria could potentially become self-sufficient and reduce costs in the long run.

Furthermore, there is an unwavering determination among Nigerian doctors and healthcare workers. Many have chosen to remain in Nigeria despite the prospect of better pay abroad. Their commitment speaks volumes about resilience and hope, and with the right support and resources, these professionals could spearhead a revolutionary leap in healthcare quality and accessibility.

Ultimately, while technology alone can't remedy all the ills of the healthcare sector in Nigeria, it serves as a critical piece of a larger strategy for progress. Healthcare reform in Nigeria is a multi-faceted endeavor that involves the diligent work of forging partnerships, facilitating educational reform, and galvanizing community action. The hope for a brighter future within the realm of Nigerian healthcare lies not just in the tools and technologies themselves, but in the persistent and innovative spirit of the Nigerian people.

As the world moves deeper into the 21st century, Nigeria has the potential to pivot from its current limitations and chart a course towards a robust and equitable healthcare system. With clear vision, ample investment, and unwavering commitment to improvement, the country's healthcare landscape can transform, reflecting not only the aspirations of Nigerian health workers but the nation's inherent capacity to innovate and overcome adversity.

Chapter 8:
Surviving on Sacrifice: Personal Stories of Nigerian Doctors

In Chapter 8, we delve into the heart-rending narratives that speak to the resilience and dedication of Nigerian doctors, enduring amidst a system strained to its limits. Behind the statistics and systemic analyses lie the real-life struggles of these medical professionals, marked by personal sacrifice and an unwavering commitment to their calling. Each story serves as a sobering reminder of the harsh realities faced daily: long hours compounded by the emotional and physical toll of conducting high-stakes medical care with woefully inadequate resources. These accounts are not mere anecdotal footnotes but the living testament of those on the front lines—navigating a path through adversity with the hope of delivering care in an environment that continuously undervalues their contribution and expertise. Their voices are a clarion call for urgent reform, as their testimonies shine a spotlight on the noble endeavor to uphold the tenets of their Hippocratic oath, despite insurmountable odds.

Daily Struggles and Triumphs

Navigating the labyrinth of Nigeria's healthcare system, doctors face an uphill battle each day. Their grueling routines comprise not just medical challenges, but also systemic hurdles that test their resolve. Pervasive shortages mean that a Nigerian doctor's day is too often framed by improvisation—stitching together solutions with scant supplies, all while managing an ever-swelling tide of patients. Despite these obstacles, there are silent victories—a precise diagnosis in spite of inadequate equipment, a life saved by sheer determination and skill, or even the simple gratitude of a healed child's smile. These triumphs become personal beacons of hope that illuminate the oft-overlooked strength and resilience required to practice medicine in such demanding conditions. For every moment of frustration, there exists a counterpoint of profound professional fulfillment, capturing the paradox that underpins the daily lives of these steadfast guardians of health.

The Emotional and Physical Toll

The impact of being a doctor in Nigeria is not merely financial—it claws deeper, into the very wellbeing of those on the front lines. When we delve into the lives of Nigerian doctors, we see individuals who endure a relentless barrage of emotional and physical challenges due to the state of healthcare in their country.

The demanding nature of the profession anywhere in the world is well documented, but in Nigeria, the situation reaches a critical point. Continuous long shifts become the norm rather than the exception, with little respite or support. Where in some countries there are defined work hours with occasional overtime, Nigerian doctors can find themselves on duty for stretches that profoundly disrupt their circadian rhythms and personal lives.

Physically, the effects are palpable. Exhaustion takes its toll. A tired doctor becomes one who is more prone to mistakes, whose hands may shake during a surgical procedure, or whose decision-making is impaired. And this physical toll compounds over time, becoming an occupational hazard that is far less visible than needle-stick injuries or the risk of contracting infections from patients, but equally as dangerous.

Mentally and emotionally, the burden is equally crushing. A pervasive sense of frustration gnaws at the psyche of these medical professionals. They are often forced to watch patients suffer or even pass away, not because their conditions are untreatable, but because the necessary infrastructure, equipment, or medications are simply not available. To desire to heal, but to be impotent in the face of systemic failure, takes a profound emotional toll on any empathetic individual.

Sadly, the rigors of such a profession in Nigeria also strain relationships. Marriages and partnerships strain under the pressure of absenteeism and the emotional baggage that doctors carry home. Celebrations are missed, children grow up with an absent parent, and ironically, doctors may fail to be there for their own families' health emergencies because they are attending to those of others.

The overwhelming workload and its associated stress often lead to psychological struggles. Cases of burnout, depression, and anxiety are not uncommon among Nigerian doctors. The mental health stigma, however, creates a barrier to seeking effective help, and many grapple with their demons in silence, an isolating and perilous endeavor.

Furthermore, the violence that healthcare workers sometimes encounter at their workplace in Nigeria is a grim reality. Doctors face threats, and even physical harm from aggrieved family members of patients, which adds a layer of fear to an already challenging working environment.

Within the hospitals, the chaos can seem unending. The clamor of overcrowded wards, the constant demands for attention, and the frustration of knowing that better outcomes are often a distant dream, leave scars that are not easily healed. Compassion fatigue sets in, where doctors become desensitized to the suffering that surrounds them, not out of cruelty, but as a coping mechanism to protect their own wellbeing.

This high-stress environment also leads to a breakdown in camaraderie among healthcare workers. The high stakes and pressure cook even the strongest team dynamics, sometimes leading to conflict and decreased collaboration, further eroding the quality of patient care, and amplifying the emotional distress of the doctors involved.

The absence of a robust support system from the government and the medical community intensifies the issue. Unlike in countries where doctors have access to peer support programs, counseling services, and mental health days, Nigerian physicians often face their battles unsupported. And those who seek assistance outside their workplace must do so with their already meager salaries, making such essential services out of reach for many.

Doctors trained in Nigeria are among some of the brightest minds, possessing skills honed through rigorous education and training programs. However, when confronted with the stark limitations of their work environment, the emotional wound of underachievement begins to fester. They are acutely aware of what they could accomplish in better circumstances, and this knowledge serves as a constant reminder of their constrained reality.

Despite these challenges, Nigerian doctors show an incredible resilience that is worthy of admiration. Their dedication to their patients often goes beyond the call of duty. They are more than just doctors—they are pillars in their communities, providing hope and solace even in the darkest of times. Their sacrifices form the bedrock upon which Nigeria's healthcare system precariously rests.

To measure the full depth of the emotional and physical toll on Nigerian doctors is an intricate task, as each individual carries their burden differently. Nonetheless, this chapter paints a grim reality of the sacrifice these professionals make. It's a call to acknowledge their plight, to consider the latent costs of their unyielding dedication, and to advocate for a healthcare environment that supports, rather than depletes, those who are committed to healing others.

As we reflect on these narratives, it is clear that the emotional and physical well-being of Nigerian doctors is not merely an individual concern but a national crisis. A healthy society is only as stable as its healthcare providers, and when they are crumbling under undue pressure, the entire healthcare structure teeters on the brink of collapse. Thus, it becomes imperative to discuss solutions not just for the sake of the doctors, but for the future of public health in Nigeria.

Chapter 9:
The Slippery Slope to Medical Misdiagnosis

Imagine the perils of navigating a steep incline, slick with the uncertainties of insufficient healthcare infrastructure—it's a fitting metaphor for the troubling ascent many Nigerians face towards proper medical diagnosis. Tainted by system-wide stresses—the blight of inadequate salaries deterring the country's most able doctors, threadbare training pushing physicians to the brink of their capabilities—these factors steepen the slope towards misdiagnosis. Is it the doctor, weary from juggling too many cases, who overlooks a crucial symptom, or the outdated equipment that fails to capture what a more advanced apparatus might catch? While Nigerian doctors battle to provide the best care, they're hampered by battered system foundations, where the shortfall in their paychecks reflects the gaping holes in patient safety nets. As we delve into the web of causes behind medical misdiagnoses, we see the dire consequences unfold: patient distrust, worsening health outcomes, and the indefatigable pressure on an already strained workforce. Yet, amidst the cascade of challenges, strategies for improvement glimmer with promise, waiting for robust support and an overhaul of a system that can't afford to fail those it's meant to heal.

Causes and Consequences

The journey into the depths of medical misdiagnosis in Nigeria is rife with systemic pitfalls. Lack of adequate training, where medical professionals grapple with outdated information and practices, is a significant contributor. Yet, there's more to the story. The alarmingly low salaries of Nigerian doctors create a domino effect that diminishes motivation and attracts fewer aspirants to the field, which, in turn, correlates with increased diagnostic errors. Additionally, the scarcity of resources—both human and material—exacerbates the likelihood of misdiagnosis, as doctors face insurmountable pressure to serve more patients than they can handle. The consequences of such a constrained system are grave, leading to patient distrust, the potential for irreversible health damage, and, at times, fatalities that could have been avoided. This section uncovers the multifaceted nature of causes while shedding light on the dire outcomes that beset patients and erode the fabric of Nigerian healthcare.

Strategies for Improvement

When considering the landscape of healthcare challenges in Nigeria, particularly the propensity for medical misdiagnosis, we must consider strategic avenues that can lead to meaningful change. This section offers a compendium of tailored strategies that target the very nucleus of improvement in the health sector. These strategies are not stand-alone solutions; rather, they are interconnected pathways that, when combined, may forge a more formidable and accurate healthcare system in Nigeria.

To commence, the establishment of a standardized protocol for diagnosis across all levels of healthcare service provision is paramount. This involves creating comprehensive guidelines that can be disseminated and enforced throughout the Nigerian medical community. By aligning diagnostic procedures, we reduce the variances that contribute to misdiagnosis while bolstering the consistency and quality of care delivered.

Investment in training and continuous education for healthcare professionals must become a non-negotiable pillar of the Nigerian healthcare system. Regular workshops, seminars, and synchronous learning opportunities provide doctors with up-to-date information on best practices and emerging medical trends, ensuring their diagnostic acumen remains sharp and well-informed.

Another critical measure is strengthening the healthcare infrastructure to support accurate and timely diagnoses. This not only entails the modernization of medical facilities but also equipping them with the necessary tools to effectively carry out diagnostics, such as improved laboratory equipment, imaging technology, and electronic health records systems.

The integration of telemedicine platforms can play a significant role in this upgrade, providing remote regions with access to specialist consultations and second opinions, which are crucial in the battle against misdiagnosis. By collapsing distance and time barriers, telemedicine enhances the capacity of physicians to reach conclusive and precise diagnoses.

We also can't overlook the power of public-private partnerships in revitalizing the diagnostic landscape in Nigeria. Collaboration between governmental bodies and private entities could result in substantial financial and technological investments that are direly needed in the healthcare sector.

Furthermore, creating a receptive environment for feedback and error reporting within healthcare institutions is vital. This system would encourage the candid reporting and analysis of diagnostic errors, which is instrumental in learning and preventing future misdiagnoses. Effective reporting mechanisms also cultivate a culture of transparency and accountability.

Moving to the fiscal aspect, fair and incentivizing remuneration for healthcare workers can drastically boost morale and reduce the likelihood of medical oversights. As we have ascertained, the current salary standards can diminish motivation and lead to subpar patient care. Thus, revising the pay scale of doctors to align with international standards is a step towards retaining talent and enhancing diagnostic reliability.

In addition to remuneration, addressing the emotional and physical toll on healthcare providers through support systems — such as counseling, stress management programs, and work-life balance initiatives — is urgent. A healthcare provider in good mental and physical health is far more likely to perform accurate diagnoses.

We must also encourage patient empowerment and education, as an informed patient populace contributes significantly to improved health outcomes. Educating patients about their right to second opinions and understanding their symptoms and possible conditions directly aids in minimizing misdiagnoses.

Implementing robust quality control measures is another technique to enforce and monitor the standards of diagnostic procedures comprehensively. These controls should encompass regular audits, peer reviews, and accreditation processes to ensure facilities and personnel adhere to high-quality diagnostic services.

Furthermore, establishing specialized diagnostic centers that focus on complex and rare conditions could serve as hubs of expertise and provide validation for challenging cases. This would considerably relieve the general practice burden and create a centralized source of knowledge and experience.

Nigerian medical research endeavors should also receive a significant impetus, as domestic research can unveil localized trends in misdiagnosis and provide targeted insights. Additionally, participating in international research collaborations can introduce Nigerian doctors to global best practices and innovative diagnostic methodologies.

On the policy front, concerted efforts must be made to eliminate corruption and mismanagement within the healthcare sector. This requires stringent governance, accountability, and the will to enact punitive measures against those who violate the integrity of healthcare delivery.

Finally, embracing a multidisciplinary approach to healthcare can aid in comprehensive patient assessment and in reducing the risk of misdiagnosis. Encouraging cross-specialty consultations and collaborative case evaluations ensures that a patient benefits from diverse medical perspectives, leading to more accurate and thorough diagnoses.

In summary, through a confluence of educational revamps, infrastructural enhancements, equitable salaries, and policy reforms, Nigeria can initiate a robust and lasting transformation of its healthcare diagnostic landscape. Such multipronged efforts can translate into a future where every patient receives the correct diagnosis, effective treatment, and the opportunity for a healthier life.

Chapter 10:
The Pharmaceutical Dilemma:
Availability and Affordability

A mid the expansive narrative of Nigeria's healthcare system, with its undulating challenges and the steadfast spirit of its medical practitioners, the subject of pharmaceuticals emerges as both a beacon of hope and a source of despair. This chapter delves into the vexing complexity of drug availability and affordability, where life-saving medications all too often dangle just beyond the reach of those in dire need. In Nigeria's case, the reliance on imported pharmaceuticals creates a perilous dependency that entwines with the pervasive issue of counterfeit drugs—a shadowy menace delivering false hope and real danger. As we examine the intricate dynamics that govern this sector, it becomes clear that the struggle for health sovereignty is not just about managing symptoms, but about finding a remedy for a system in critical condition. This journey through the pharmaceutical labyrinth paints a picture of a society grasping for solutions to assure that the right medicine—at the right price—is in the hands of those who need it most.

Import Dependence and Local Production Challenges

In Nigeria, the availability and affordability of pharmaceuticals are pivotal to the healthcare sector's efficacy. The pharmaceutical dilemma that stitches through the fabric of Nigerian healthcare is, in large part, a problem of import dependence and local production challenges. Far from being an issue of simple economics, this predicament impacts lives on a personal scale every day, putting a harsh spotlight on the already strained healthcare system.

The nation's heavy reliance on imported pharmaceuticals is a multifaceted problem. On one hand, the global pharmaceutical market offers products that might not be produced domestically in Nigeria. However, this reliance breeds a vulnerability—a disruption in the global supply chain can lead to critical shortages in-country. The COVID-19 pandemic has made this particularly clear, presenting scenarios wherein medications and vaccines were, and continue to be, desperately awaited.

Local production of pharmaceuticals in Nigeria is beleaguered with its own set of hurdles. Insufficient investment in the sector translates to a limited scale of operations. Factories that could produce essential drugs often lack the technological know-how or the capital to procure the necessary machinery. Furthermore, the workforce required to upscale local production is not readily available, due in part to the education system which struggles to produce graduates with the requisite skills in pharmaceutical technology.

The cost of local production also presents an economic enigma. Pharmaceutical companies that manage to produce medicines domestically often incur higher costs than those importing similar drugs. These increased costs result from a combination of factors including high electricity costs due to power instability, the expense of importing active pharmaceutical ingredients, and the often prohibitive cost of quality assurance and certification.

Quality control is yet another formidable barrier. Nigeria's National Agency for Food and Drug Administration and Control (NAFDAC) sets stringent standards for pharmaceutical production. While these regulations are crucial for ensuring safety, they can stymie local production when manufacturers lack the resources to meet them. This not only affects local businesses but also the healthcare system's capacity to provide affordable, effective medication.

In addition to these economic and regulatory constraints, local manufacturers face competition from international pharmaceutical giants. These entities, with their massive economies of scale, can often produce and sell drugs at lower prices than their Nigerian counterparts. This competitive disadvantage discourages investment in the local pharmaceutical industry, leading to a vicious cycle of underdevelopment and dependency.

Financing is another critical element. Nigerian pharmaceutical companies frequently cite difficulties in securing loans with reasonable interest rates to sustain and expand their operations. Where financing is obtainable, the cost implications sometimes drive the final product's price up, again making it difficult to compete with imported alternatives.

Government policy has sometimes acted as both a cure and a curse in this scenario. Protectionist measures aimed at boosting local production can have unintended consequences, such as the exclusion of Nigeria from favorable trade agreements, while tax breaks and subsidies aimed at stimulating local industry are often not targeted effectively, or funded insufficiently, to make a tangible impact.

The challenges of local pharmaceutical production aren't solely institutional or economic; they're interwoven with societal issues as well. Health literacy in Nigeria is an overlooked dimension that affects local production. A population well-informed about the importance of supporting domestic manufacturers might favor local products, even at a higher cost, due to their guaranteed quality and the economic benefits of supporting local businesses. However, this is not typically the case, as imported products are often perceived as superior.

Infrastructure deficiencies play a critical role too. The inadequate transportation network hamstrings distribution channels for local producers, translating into limited market access and increased costs. Meanwhile, logistics issues can lead to storage problems, which can affect the quality and shelf-life of pharmaceutical products.

Energy supply is erratic and unreliable. Manufacturers that require constant power for their operations are thus forced to seek backup solutions, which can lead to increased carbon footprints and additional operational costs. The ripple effect is significant: every additional generator and every liter of diesel further escalates the cost of local medicines.

Environmental factors cannot be discounted either. Nigeria's temperate climate, characterized by high humidity and temperature, dictates a need for stable and controlled manufacturing and storage conditions to ensure drug efficacy. The cost of establishing such facilities—equipped with the correct HVAC and humidity control systems—adds another layer of financial burden on producers.

In contemplating the future, substantial investments in research and development (R&D) are essential for the growth of the domestic pharmaceutical industry. R&D can lead to the development of new drugs better suited to the needs of Nigerians, as well as improved production processes that can reduce costs. Sadly, the current levels of investment in this area are woefully inadequate.

One cannot discuss these production challenges without touching upon the workforce that powers it—or the lack thereof. With doctors and healthcare workers seeking greener pastures abroad, the brain drain phenomenon has left the nation in a precarious situation. Those with pharmaceutical expertise are also part of this exodus, leaving a gap in both the conception and execution of pharmaceutical manufacturing.

To enhance local production capabilities and reduce dependency on imports, a concerted effort must be made by stakeholders within and outside the government. Complementing better policy-making with consistent funding, incentivizing R&D, and enhancing the operational environment are steps that need to be taken. Only a holistic approach that tackles the multifaceted challenges facing the local pharmaceutical sector can lead to a sustainable improvement in the availability and affordability of medicines for Nigerians, bridging the gap to a healthier Nigeria.

The Menace of Counterfeit Medications

In the vast landscape of Nigeria's healthcare struggles, the issue of counterfeit medications presents a particularly insidious threat. The situation is dire: a lethal cascade effect where patients, seeking relief from their ailments, are instead met with remedies that range from ineffective to downright dangerous.

The problem of counterfeit medication is far more than an abstract concept—it's a daily gambit for health and survival. Picture this: you're a patient with a mild fever and cough. You venture to a pharmacy, where the promise of a cure comes in a small package. You take the medicine, expecting to feel better, but the illness lingers, or worse, complications develop. Trust in medicine is crucial, yet in Nigeria, that trust is continuously eroded by the specter of counterfeits.

Why is Nigeria fertile ground for this menace? The answers lie partly in the country's over-reliance on imported pharmaceuticals. With local production facing an uphill battle—marked by underfunding and outdated technology—the market is flooded with imported alternatives that can sometimes be fakes.

These counterfeit drugs sneak into the supply chain, shadowed by inadequate regulatory systems that struggle to ensure quality control. In practice, the checks and balances that should safeguard the pharmaceutical market are riddled with lapses, often due to corruption and bureaucratic inefficiencies.

The financial allure for counterfeiters is undeniable. They operate on the principle of high profit at low cost, leveraging the desperation of a population in need of affordable medications. The price of genuine drugs is often out of reach for many Nigerians, which creates a void that counterfeiters are all too willing to fill.

So, what's the magnitude of this problem? Surveys and studies suggest that up to 70% of drugs in some Nigerian markets may be counterfeit or substandard. This is not just a number; it's a reflection of actual lives at stake. For those suffering from life-threatening conditions such as malaria or HIV/AIDS, these fake medicines can be a death sentence.

Patients aren't the only ones suffering; doctors are also at a precipice. Imagine endlessly studying and training to heal, only to be undermined by ineffective drugs. The already meager salaries of these professionals are a stark contrast to the fortunes amassed by the purveyors of fake drugs.

While the spotlight often lands on anti-malarials and antibiotics as common counterfeits, the issue permeates almost every category of medicine. Painkillers, diabetes medications, and even treatments for cancer—none are immune to falsification.

The economic implications are vast but often overshadowed by the human cost. Counterfeit drugs erode trust in health systems, discourage patients from seeking care, and contribute to a cycle of poverty and sickness as people spend their limited resources on treatments that won't work.

Addressing this menace isn't straightforward. It requires a multi-faceted approach, including strengthening regulatory frameworks, increasing public awareness, improving access to affordable and authentic medications, and empowering law enforcement agencies to crack down on counterfeit networks.

Moreover, combating the counterfeit drug problem can't happen in isolation. The relationship between drug quality and healthcare outcomes stresses the importance of enhancing overall healthcare systems, from salary structures to infrastructure development and beyond.

In Nigeria, the call to action is clear: safeguard the health of the population by assuring the medications they depend on are legitimate and effective. It's a matter of urgency; it's a matter of preserving the integrity of healthcare and, ultimately, saving lives.

As we delve deeper into the plight of Nigeria's healthcare quagmire, the counterfeit medication crisis presents a sobering reminder. It highlights the interconnectedness of issues—a reminder that solutions to healthcare challenges must be comprehensive, addressing both the availability and the authenticity of life-saving medicines.

In the following chapters, we will explore other facets of Nigeria's healthcare puzzle. But let it be known, the menace of counterfeit medications is more than a chapter; it's a recurring narrative threading through the very fabric of Nigeria's healthcare system—a predicament that calls for immediate attention and unwavering resolve.

Chapter 11:
Partnerships and Aid: Domestic
and International Efforts

In the quest to fortify Nigeria's ailing healthcare system, the role of partnerships and international aid can't be understated. Within this intricate dance of support, NGOs alongside foreign governments inject much-needed vigor into the veins of Nigerian health services. Moving beyond handouts, these synergetic relationships are crucial, striving to address not only the glaring shortfalls in medical supplies and infrastructure but also in empowering the country's medical professionals whose salaries often do not reflect the critical nature of their work. Such collaborations, however, come laden with questions of effectiveness and the sustainability of their outcomes. As this chapter unfolds, we'll navigate the multifaceted dynamics of these partnerships, peeking beneath the surface of benevolence to assess whether these efforts are mere stopgaps or stepping stones to a robust healthcare future for Nigeria.

NGOs and Foreign Assistance

Amid the patchwork efforts to address Nigeria's healthcare deficiencies, NGOs and foreign aid play pivotal roles, injecting much-needed vigor into a system beleaguered by limited resources and dwindling morale among health professionals. Dynamic partnerships between local initiatives and international organizations are often the lifeblood for rural clinics where government support fades into the background. Compelled by the struggle of Nigerian doctors whose livelihoods barely keep pace with their commitment to heal, global entities endeavour to bolster salaries and sustain operations. Still, these are but temporary salves to a system craving more than a monetary fix; the foreign assistance speaks to an ethos of communal responsibility while raising an implicit question about the longevity of such aid in transcending the complexity of healthcare challenges. By providing equipment, training, and financial supplements, these organizations illuminate the power of collective action yet also remind us of the importance of building capacity for self-reliance within Nigeria's health sectors.

Evaluating the Effectiveness and Sustainability

of the efforts to improve healthcare in Nigeria demands a rigorous and multi-dimensional approach. It is pivotal to scrutinize both domestic and international interventions, not only for their immediate outcomes but for their long-term impacts on the medical landscape. The relentless brain drain of doctors, exacerbated by poor pay, has only intensified the need for sustainable solutions.

One must critically look at the partnerships and aid provided to the health sector in Nigeria. The influx of Non-Governmental Organizations (NGOs) and international assistance is seen as a beacon of hope amidst the crisis. However, their success isn't solely measured by the number of clinics built or the quantity of supplies provided. Rather, the sustainability of these programs and their integration into the existing health system are key indicators of their effectiveness.

NGOs often step in to fill the void left by governmental shortcomings, but without careful coordination, these efforts can lead to a parallel system that might crumble once the NGOs withdraw. It's imperative to work alongside local health authorities, ensuring knowledge transfer and capacity building. This approach empowers Nigerian doctors and medical staff, enabling them to sustain operations in the long term.

Financial assistance from abroad also warrants scrutiny, particularly with respect to how it's allocated. Funding must be utilized effectively, targeting the root causes of healthcare deficiencies rather than just the symptoms. For example, while increasing doctors' salaries can be a powerful incentive to stay, this strategy must be coupled with investments in training and infrastructure to enhance overall systemic resilience.

The sustainability of intervention efforts also involves ensuring that they are culturally sensitive and appropriate. Programs designed without substantial local input risk being ill-suited to the communities they intend to serve. Involving Nigerian doctors in designing and implementing these initiatives is crucial, as they intimately understand the unique challenges and needs of their patients.

Too often have well-meant aid projects faltered due to a lack of alignment with local healthcare policies or a failure to adequately anticipate the maintenance and operational requirements after the initial setup. Ongoing support and the training of local healthcare workers can do much to mitigate these risks, securing the longevity of healthcare improvements.

The measurement of success has often been limited to quantitative data, such as the number of patients treated or facilities opened. However, a qualitative understanding is just as important. The perception of improved healthcare among Nigerian doctors and patients is an indispensable part of evaluating the effectiveness of aid. Their satisfaction and the improvement in the quality of care are the true measures of progress.

Moreover, the financial sustainability of health initiatives hinges on creating robust economic models. Over-reliance on external funding exposes the Nigerian healthcare system to the vagaries of geopolitical shifts and the whims of foreign donors. Thus, establishing a self-sufficient revenue model, possibly through public-private partnerships, can create resilient financial frameworks to support the healthcare system.

Reliable supply chains for medication and equipment are a cornerstone of sustainability. Initiatives must address the pharmaceutical conundrum, improving the availability and affordability of authentic medications. Strengthening local production capabilities, alongside stringent oversight to prevent the proliferation of counterfeit drugs, is a particularly important aspect of a sustainable health sector.

Another aspect often neglected in the realm of sustainability is environmental considerations. Medical facilities must be built with not just efficacy in mind, but also efficiency. Energy-saving practices and waste reduction measures play a crucial part in ensuring that the health sector contributes to the well-being of Nigerians without depleting the country's natural resources.

Lastly, the definition of sustainability in healthcare extends to maintaining mental and physical well-being for healthcare providers. Nigeria's doctors often face burnout due to excessive workloads and stressful work environments. Sustainable healthcare systems, therefore, must also create conditions that prevent the erosion of healthcare workers' well-being.

To sum up, evaluating effectiveness and sustainability is a continuous process needing robust monitoring mechanisms. It requires critical awareness of potential pitfalls and imaginative strategies to circumvent them, ensuring that the assistance provided today doesn't become the dependency of tomorrow.

The discourse on these matters must remain open and adaptive, guided by best practices and a commitment to long-term improvement. Indeed, the durability of Nigeria's health reforms will be determined by the vigilance and dedication of stakeholders at every level, from international partners to local doctors.

As the narrative of Nigerian healthcare continues to unfold, the lessons garnered from evaluating the effectiveness and sustainability of current efforts will illuminate the path to a hoped-for future of health security and prosperity. Achieving this vision requires not just constructive intervention but meaningful transformation that stands the test of time.

Chapter 12:
Visions of a Healthier Future:
Reform and Innovation

As we have navigated the challenges and nuances of Nigeria's healthcare situation in previous chapters, it becomes essential to pivot towards a landscape of reform and innovation that could herald a brighter epoch for the health sector. Envisioning a healthier future for Nigeria encompasses both a recognition of the pioneering case studies that have managed to thrive despite constraints, and a strategic roadmap for systemic changes that are both visionary and pragmatically rooted in the current socio-economic fabric. Tackling the dire salary situation of doctors and healthcare professionals calls for a multipronged approach that values talent, provides opportunities for professional growth, and secures financial incentives aligned with global standards. With the prevailing exodus of medical talent, it is imperative for policy shapers to architect frameworks that harness the potential of technological advancement, foster partnerships with the private sectors, and ultimately ensure accessibility, affordability, and quality care that every Nigerian deserves.

Case Studies of Success

The healthcare landscape in Nigeria, often painted in stark terms of deficit and need, is also home to stories of success that illuminate the potential pathways for a transformative future. Let's pivot the lens to these beacons of hope as exemplified by pioneering programs, resilient healthcare professionals, and the impactful use of technology, which collectively contribute compelling evidence that positive change is possible.

An inspiring instance is the telemedicine initiative that sprang from the necessity to address rural healthcare access. A nonprofit, leveraging a combination of satellite communications and mobile technology, has connected remote village clinics with urban medical centers. The program enables remote diagnostics and has shown significant improvement in primary care, particularly for maternal health—a key indicator of overall healthcare quality.

Another success story is etched in the adoption of electronic medical records within select hospitals. This innovation reduced administrative burdens significantly, freeing up more time for direct patient care, and dramatically cut down on record-keeping errors. Although scaling this across the nation poses substantial challenges, the instanced gains suggest it's a worthy endeavor.

Further afield, a teaching hospital in Southwestern Nigeria became a national frontrunner when it introduced a Continuing Medical Education (CME) program designed to enhance the skills of its medical staff. It prioritized advanced training in fields where Nigeria suffers a critical shortage of expertise. The success of this program outlines the benefits of investment in the education and retention of medical professionals within the country.

Financial constraints can often stifle innovation, yet even modest budgets have yielded impressive results. For instance, a government hospital refurbished its equipment using a combination of grants and low-interest loans. By circumventing the need for expensive, brand-new technologies, it increased its operational capacity while conservatively managing resources.

One must not overlook the individual triumphs that comprise the collective success of the healthcare system. Stories of Nigerian doctors forming community health outreaches fill the lives of the underserved with hope. These outreaches, facilitated by volunteer work and donated supplies, showcase the relentless dedication of Nigerian health professionals to their compatriots, translating into improved community wellbeing.

Amidst these stirring narratives, a public-private partnership in the north of the country illustrates the synergy that can be achieved when governmental support aligns with private sector efficiency. Together they have rebuilt a local clinic, modernizing its infrastructure, and subsequently reducing patient wait times while increasing the availability of essential medications.

Grassroots efforts, too, deserve applause as they reflect the powerful change that can emerge from citizen initiative. A coalition of women's groups mobilized to promote vaccination, receiving training and support from international organizations. Their work has seen a significant uptick in immunization rates, underscoring the value of community-led health interventions.

Health education, a preventative weapon often under-utilized, flourished in a campaign that harnessed the power of radio and social media. Targeting communicable diseases, it raised awareness and disarmed myths and misinformation, consequently decreasing incidence rates of diseases such as cholera and Lassa fever.

One cannot talk about healthcare without considering the facilities. A renovation project, purely funded from the hospital's internally generated revenue, displays an exceptional model of self-reliance. This effort not only provided upgraded facilities but ended up instilling a deep-seated pride and ownership among staff and patients who witnessed the transformation.

On the technology front, an indigenously developed mobile health app has distinguished itself by providing rural users with health tips, reminders for medication, and alerts on outbreaks. The app's user base has grown steadily, its expanding reach a testament to the potential for homegrown solutions to penetrate areas conventionally overlooked by larger tech ventures.

In the sphere of specialist care, a clinic specializing in diabetic retinopathy instituted a screening and treatment protocol unheard of in its region. With an emphasis on early intervention, the clinic has prevented blindness in thousands, establishing a replicable model of specialty care even within resource-poor settings.

Then there's the saga of one state hospital's approach to maternal mortality. By establishing a blood donation drive and emergency obstetric care training for its staff, the hospital significantly slashed its maternal death rates, propelling the conversation on maternal health into the national agenda.

Metrics, though not the most enthralling aspect of healthcare, have been pivotal in one regional health department's strategy. By meticulously analyzing data, they were able to allocate resources efficiently, profoundly impacting infant and child mortality rates in their jurisdiction.

Despite being a beacon of hope, each successful case is also a reminder that the capacity for further success isn't evenly distributed or fully realized. Documenting and disseminating the frameworks of these successes is as critical as sustaining them—and therein lies the promise of a healthier future for Nigeria.

On the financial side of things, a pilot project that implemented a micro-insurance health scheme allowed patients to afford care without the burden of catastrophic out-of-pocket expenses. The result? An increased rate of hospital visits and preventative care, fostering a healthier community and proving that financial models for healthcare in Nigeria can indeed be reformed.

These vignettes of success serve as the cornerstone for the chapters that follow, where we explore not just the visionaries behind these achievements but also delineate a roadmap for systemic changes that can expand these island of excellence into a continent of progress in Nigerian healthcare.

Roadmap for Systemic Changes

As we venture further into our exploration of a healthier future for Nigeria, we now turn our focus to the roadmap for systemic changes. These are not mere suggestions; they are vital strategies that if implemented, could revolutionize the healthcare system in Nigeria, addressing issues that range from infrastructural gaps to the crippling doctor exodus.

The foundational step in this journey must be the consolidation of health sector reform policies. For too long, policies have been fragmented, piecemeal, and sometimes conflicting. A cohesive policy document, with input from healthcare professionals, policy experts, and community representatives, will set the stage for a harmonized system.

At the heart of these policies should be the prioritization of human resources. This means not only increasing the salaries of doctors to competitive levels but also providing them with opportunities for continuous education and professional development. Adequate remuneration and self-improvement options are key to retaining medical talent within the country.

Infrastructure investment cannot be overlooked. It's critical to provide healthcare facilities with state-of-the-art equipment and to ensure that these tools are maintained. Reliable electricity, clean water, and essential medical machinery are non-negotiable for the delivery of quality care.

Recognizing the vast urban-rural divide, a concerted effort to delegate resources and healthcare workers to rural areas is necessary. These communities often bear the brunt of neglect, and a balanced distribution of resources will address the inequity in healthcare access.

Streamlining the patient-to-doctor ratio is equally crucial. This can be tackled from multiple angles: increasing the intake and training of medical students, employing more healthcare workers, and leveraging telemedicine to extend the reach of existing practitioners.

On the policy front, it's paramount to combat corruption and bureaucratic inefficiency in the healthcare sector. Instituting transparent processes and stringent oversight mechanisms will foster a culture of accountability and ensure that funds allocated for health are used effectively.

Embracing technological innovation could bridge the gap in diagnosis and treatment. With a landscape ripe for digital health solutions, Nigeria can integrate mobile health apps, electronic health records, and telehealth services to bolster the health system's efficiency.

Preventive healthcare should be a key fixture in the reform agenda. Public health campaigns, vaccination drives, and community health education can diminish the burden of diseases and reduce overall healthcare costs.

Reform must also extend to the pharmaceutical sector. Incentivizing and supporting local drug production, while enhancing regulations to thwart the circulation of counterfeit medications, will strengthen the pharmaceutical supply chain and ensure medication quality and availability.

Furthermore, addressing the systemic challenges inherent in misdiagnosis requires standardization of diagnostic protocols and bolstering laboratory services. With better diagnostics, the risks of incorrect treatment and patient suffering can be significantly lowered.

International partnerships and aid play a unique role in the health sector and must be harnessed effectively. Strategic collaborations with NGOs and foreign health agencies can offer a wealth of resources and expertise. However, these relationships should be built on the principles of sustainability and local ownership.

Finally, advocating for stronger healthcare protection through insurance coverage will alleviate the financial burden on patients. Expanding coverage and simplifying the claims process would ensure that more Nigerians can access and afford essential healthcare services.

Collectively, these steps form a comprehensive approach to overhauling the healthcare system in Nigeria. From infrastructure to human resource development, policy reform to technological innovation, this is a multi-faceted endeavor that requires commitment, investment, and a relentless pursuit of excellence. The vision of a healthier Nigeria is attainable, but it demands action that is immediate, structured, and resolute.

It is through these efforts that we can envisage a future where Nigerian doctors thrive in their homeland, equipped with resources and respect, and where every citizen has access to quality healthcare. The task ahead is monumental, no doubt, but the rewards—a robust health system and a healthier population—are well worth the endeavor.

Conclusion

In tracing the contours of Nigeria's healthcare system through the preceding chapters, a mosaic of burdens and challenges has emerged, but so too have flickers of resilience and the potential for reform. The healthcare landscape in Nigeria stands at a critical juncture, where the pressing need for substantial change is as undeniable as it is urgent.

The constellation of issues—from the scarcity of resources and equipment to the significant flux of medical talent leaving the country—paints a sobering picture of the Nigerian healthcare system. Providing adequate care to the populace seems like an insurmountable task when scrutinizing the depleted ranks of the medical staff juxtaposed with the patient-to-doctor ratio that strains believability.

Financial insecurity has bred a silent crisis among Nigerian doctors, whose remuneration pales in comparison to their international peers. This has not just stoked the fire of migration but has also chipped away at the morale of those who choose to stay against daunting odds. The outcome is a workforce continually on the brink, maneuvering through exhaustion and disillusionment to provide basic care.

Rural populations stand particularly vulnerable, facing a gaping divide in access to healthcare, exacerbated by urban-centric policies and infrastructure development. Meanwhile, systemic corruption and bureaucratic lethargy have calcified into formidable barriers against the effective distribution of aid and the efficient management of resources. These are but a few of the critical areas we've explored where vast improvements are obligatory.

Against this backdrop of challenges, the stories of Nigerian doctors themselves shine a poignant light on the harsh realities of the medical profession in the country. From their sacrifices to their undying commitment, these narratives highlight the individual and collective struggle to keep the hope of accessible healthcare alive.

Medical misdiagnosis and the pharmaceutical quagmire of counterfeit medication are symptoms of deeper regulatory and oversight maladies. It's a telling sign that when trust in medical systems falters, the well-being of a nation follows suit. And yet, even here amidst the mire of malfunction, there are steps that can be taken, solutions that can be implemented to track a path towards improvement.

It bears mentioning the tireless work of NGOs and aid organizations that have been pivotal in propping up Nigeria's healthcare system. These partnerships, while invaluable, also highlight the quandary of dependency that raises questions about the sustainability and self-sufficiency of healthcare provision.

Efforts towards technological innovation hold promise, potentially bridging gaps in diagnosis and treatment that have long plagued the system. It is imperative to explore these avenues with vigor and support them with policies that foster an environment ripe for technological uptake and indigenous innovation.

Real reform, as suggested in the chapters of this narrative, lies in the hands of policymakers, healthcare professionals, and civil society. Wielding the roadmap for systemic changes, these stakeholders can catalyze a transformation that is both visionary and grounded in the realities of Nigeria's current context.

Case studies from around the globe offer a lens into what could be possible if a concerted effort is directed towards comprehensive healthcare reform in Nigeria. The successes of others reveal that while the journey is arduous, it is traversable with the right mix of commitment, investment, and international collaboration.

This text concludes, but the dialogue it hopes to inspire must not. For the patients who suffer silently, for the doctors whose pleas go unheard, for the policymakers tasked with steering the course—this conversation must stay at the forefront. This is not just a call for attention; it is a call to action.

What emerges from the pages of this book is more than a mere assessment of Nigerian healthcare. It is an invocation for empathy, a rallying cry for support, and a blueprint for the potential harbored within the hearts and minds of medical professionals across the nation.

As the global community continues to grapple with healthcare challenges, the lessons from Nigeria's experience resonate far beyond its borders. The stark realities faced by the country's healthcare system underscore a universal truth: the health of a nation's people is the bedrock upon which its future is built.

To the protagonists of this narrative—the doctors of Nigeria—their endeavors merit not just acknowledgment, but wholehearted support. And to those in positions of power, the imperatives are clear: prioritize health, incentivize retention, invest in infrastructure, foster innovation, and pave the way for a healthcare system that is robust, equitable, and dignified.

In closing, let us recognize that this is a narrative that continues to unfold. It is one that we all have a stake in, for the wellness of individuals across Nigeria profoundly influences the tapestry of global health. Therefore, the pursuit of a healthier future for Nigeria should not be seen as a solitary endeavor, but as a collective ambition—a mission that is as vital as it is just.

Appendix A:
Comparative Salary Charts for Nigerian Doctors

In this appendix, we delve into the most pressing issues surrounding the compensation of Nigerian medical doctors. Given their high level of expertise and the critical nature of their work, the scrutiny of their remuneration is warranted, especially when contrasted with their international counterparts. Within these charts, we not only see numbers, but also stories—tales that echo the sentiments of a workforce fighting to maintain its dignity amidst trying conditions.

Comparing the Basics

When one examines the salary structure of Nigerian doctors, it's clear that they are compensated far less than their peers in other parts of the world. A medical doctor's salary in Nigeria starts at the lower end of the scale, with monthly earnings that are often not commensurate with their level of responsibility or the hours invested in patient care. Let's examine the figures that tell this tale more vividly.

For instance, a junior doctor in Nigeria may earn as little as $300 (USD) a month, while the same level in countries like the United Kingdom or the United States can pull in over ten times that amount. Even when considering cost of living adjustments, the chasm between the two incomes is stark. With such discrepancies, it isn't surprising that the lure of practicing abroad can resonate so powerfully with Nigerian medical professionals.

Scales of Progression

As Nigerian doctors progress within their careers, the increments in salary are minimal compared to the standard progressions one might observe internationally. Furthermore, these increases are often inconsistent and delayed due to administrative and governmental setbacks. While an experienced consultant in Nigeria might earn up to $1,200 (USD) monthly, this number visibly pales when laid side by side against a counterpart's salary in the United States, which could potentially be over $15,000 (USD).

The numbers presented here speak volumes and elucidate the disparities that fuel the migration of talent from Nigeria to lands that promise better financial remuneration and career satisfaction. This exodus is not just a loss of individuals, but a hemorrhage of skills, experience, and potentially life-saving expertise.

What the Charts Reveal

It's imperative to acknowledge that while salary charts can render a realistic picture of the economic disparity, they can't capture the entirety of the struggles Nigerian doctors face. Behind each data point is a doctor's choice between staying in their homeland to practice medicine under challenging conditions or seeking opportunities that provide a life of financial security and professional growth beyond Nigerian borders. The charts reinforce the narrative that the quality of healthcare and the healthcare workforce in Nigeria cannot be detached from the economic realities these professionals navigate daily.

In conclusion, while viewing the comparative salary charts for Nigerian doctors, it's crucial to understand they are not just reflective of financial measures but are indicative of systemic issues that need addressing if Nigeria is to retain its medical professionals and improve its healthcare system. The data serves as a clarion call for a restructuring that looks beyond numbers, towards sustainable remuneration and working conditions that dignify the invaluable service these doctors provide.

Appendix B:
List of NGOs Operating in Nigerian Healthcare

Within the landscape of Nigerian healthcare, it is the work of non-governmental organizations (NGOs) that often fills the gaps left by government inadequacies. Tirelessly working to improve conditions for both patients and healthcare professionals, these entities range from global networks to local initiatives. Each one contributes to the complex tapestry of healthcare provision in a country striving toward a brighter, healthier future.

NGOs in Nigeria face a unique set of challenges, navigating socio-economic, political, and infrastructural hurdles to deliver essential services and support. Whether they're rolling out community-based health education programs, providing training to local healthcare workers, or bringing much-needed medical supplies to under-equipped facilities, their role cannot be overstressed.

Following is an illustrative, though not exhaustive, list of non-governmental organizations which have demonstrated a sustained commitment to enhancing the state of healthcare in Nigeria:

International Health NGOs

- **Doctors Without Borders (Médecins Sans Frontières)**
- **The Bill & Melinda Gates Foundation**
- **International Committee of the Red Cross**

Local Health Initiatives

- **The Nigerian Medical Association** - While primarily an association, it also engages in non-profit activities that support healthcare delivery.

- **The Tony Elumelu Foundation** - With a focus on empowering entrepreneurs, they also support healthcare initiatives.

- **The Wellbeing Foundation Africa**

Woman and Child Health Advocates

- **Fistula Foundation Nigeria**

- **Society for Family Health Nigeria**

- **Save the Children Nigeria**

Disease-Specific Organizations

- **The Nigeria AIDS Initiative**

- **The Nigerian Cancer Society**

- **The Tuberculosis and Leprosy Control Programme**

Mental Health and Psychosocial Support Groups

- **Mental and Environmental Development Initiative for Children (MENDIC)**

- **Mental Health Foundation Nigeria**

All of these organizations and many more are integral to the fabric of healthcare in Nigeria. They work on the frontlines, at times harmoniously with government agencies and at others, supplementing where the system falls short. In addition to these, there are countless smaller NGOs and community groups whose daily efforts conjure ripples of progress throughout the nation's health corridors. In understanding their impact and reach, we move closer to a comprehensive view of the healthcare situation in Nigeria. Efforts such as these symbolize hope and action, challenging the obstacles that besiege the Nigerian healthcare system.

Appendix C:
Recommended Policy Changes for
Nigerian Healthcare System

The struggle is palpable among those who navigate the Nigerian healthcare system—patients and providers alike. Doctors weather the storm of systemic inefficiencies, and patients face the repercussions. This appendix aims to lay out a clear path for policy reform, with the hope that the suggested changes can stem the tide and restore the sanctity of healthcare provision in Nigeria.

Enhancing Financial Incentives for Medical Professionals

At the heart of a functioning healthcare system are its workers—especially the doctors at the frontline. To address the exodus of medical professionals, a pressing recommendation is the overhaul of the remuneration system. This would include substantial salary increases to combat the current disparities when compared to international pay standards, ensuring that medical professionals can live comfortably and are not swayed by opportunities abroad.

Fostering Sustainable Infrastructure Development

Infrastructure underpins both the confidence in a healthcare system and its capacity. Priority must be given to continuous improvements in hospital facilities, bolstering the procurement process for medical resources and equipment, and ensuring reliable electricity and water supply.

Investment in infrastructure not only supports better patient care but also serves as an incentive for professionals considering practicing in rural or underdeveloped urban areas. Accordingly, maintenance culture must be entrenched to protect these investments.

Streamlining Healthcare Administration

Bureaucratic efficiency is another pillar that requires strengthening. The current system suffers from policy paralysis, where actions are stifled by red tape and corruption. There's a need for transparent governance structures and stringent internal control measures within the health sectors to focus resources where they are most needed and to minimize mismanagement.

Strengthening Training and Support Systems for Physicians

The development of a robust support system for medical training is essential. Providing comprehensive resources, access to current medical research, and opportunities for continued education will ensure that doctors are well-equipped to face the evolving challenges in healthcare. Greater incentives for specialization and ongoing professional development can help to address the specific skills gaps within the Nigerian healthcare landscape.

Improving Patient-doctor Ratios

Alleviating the pressure on overburdened medical professionals requires a multipronged approach. One vital policy change would be the implementation of a strategic recruitment and training program aimed at scaling up the numbers of healthcare providers. This program would include initiatives such as scholarships and fast-tracked employment for medical school graduates to improve the staffing levels across the country.

Enhancing Technological Capabilities

The technological chasm that currently exists hampers the ability to provide contemporary care and limits Nigeria's appeal to practicing modern medicine. Investment in medical technology is crucial for diagnostic and treatment services and should be viewed as an indispensable component of healthcare reform.

Addressing Rural and Urban Healthcare Disparities

Policy changes should also explicitly address the urban-rural divide in healthcare access. This could involve the expansion of telemedicine services, mobile clinics, and incentives for doctors working in rural regions. Establishing partnership models between urban hospitals and rural clinics can also facilitate better resource allocation and knowledge sharing.

Combatting Counterfeit Medications

A secure pharmaceutical supply chain is central to safe and reliable healthcare. Strict enforcement against counterfeit medications, support for local drug manufacturing, and pricing regulations to ensure affordability are all policy initiatives that would contribute significantly to a healthier Nigeria.

Investing in Preventative Care

Focusing on preventative care through a robust public health education campaign and vaccination programs can contribute to overall societal health, reducing the burden on hospitals and clinics.

Policies that promote public health can lead to a significant decrease in preventable diseases, thus saving resources and lives.

All these policy changes can't just be aspirations. Concrete steps backed by legislation, funding, and societal support must be taken. Awaiting on the horizon is the potential for a more robust, equitable, and sustainable healthcare system, but it necessitates a willingness to tackle each of these issues with conviction and creativity. By implementing these recommendations, Nigeria can chart a course toward a future where doctors stay, patients heal, and the healthcare system becomes a beacon of hope rather than a symbol of systemic neglect.

Glossary

The journey through Nigeria's healthcare landscape reveals a complex tapestry of terms and concepts that may be unfamiliar to some. This glossary serves to demystify these terms, providing clarity and context to enhance the reader's understanding of the issues facing healthcare in Nigeria and the conditions under which doctors work. It's an essential tool to grasp the narrative woven through the previous chapters.

A

- **Access to Healthcare:** The ability of individuals to receive health services when needed, which can be influenced by various factors such as distance, cost, and availability of medical resources.

B

- **Bureaucratic Ailments:** Issues arising from inefficient or overly complex governmental procedures that hinder the delivery of healthcare services.

C

- **Comparative Analysis:** An examination of how Nigerian doctors' salaries compare with those of their international counterparts.

- **Counterfeit Medications:** Drugs that are fraudulently produced or mislabeled, often lacking the intended active ingredients, and potentially harmful.

- **Corruption:** The abuse of entrusted power for private gain, which can significantly affect the quality and distribution of healthcare resources.

E

- **Exodus:** The mass departure of medical professionals seeking better opportunities abroad, often causing a brain drain in their home country.

G

- **Government Failings:** Deficiencies in how the healthcare system is managed at the governmental level, often leading to inadequate services and resources.

H

- **Healthcare System:** The organization of people, institutions, and resources to deliver health care services to meet the health needs of target populations.

- **Hidden Costs:** Indirect or unanticipated expenses that patients incur in accessing healthcare services.

I

- **Import Dependence:** Reliance on imported products, such as pharmaceuticals, which can result in high costs and supply vulnerabilities.

- **Infrastructure Challenges:** The physical structural problems within healthcare facilities, such as inadequate buildings or lack of utilities, impeding service delivery.

- **Innovation:** The introduction of new ideas or methods in healthcare, including technology, to improve diagnosis and treatment.

M

- **Medical Misdiagnosis:** An incorrect determination of a patient's condition, which can lead to inappropriate treatment and outcomes.

N

- **NGOs:** Non-Governmental Organizations that often contribute to healthcare improvement efforts within countries like Nigeria.

P

- **Policy Paralysis:** Inability or unwillingness of policymakers to make decisions or take action, often resulting in stagnation or decline in healthcare service quality.

- **Push Factors:** Conditions within Nigeria that compel doctors to seek employment abroad, such as poor pay, working conditions, or lack of opportunities.

R

- **Resources and Equipment Shortages:** A lack of necessary supplies and medical devices that are essential for healthcare professionals to deliver proper care.

S

- **Salary:** The periodic payment received by doctors for their work and services, a central discussion point in examining their livelihoods.

T

- **Technology Gap:** The disparity between available medical technologies in Nigeria and those in more developed healthcare systems.

The threads that tie the embattled Nigerian healthcare system and the tenacity of its medical professionals are many and varied. By understanding these terms, readers can better navigate the nuances of this critical issue and appreciate the gravity of what is at stake for countless individuals within the country.